MW01109680

Being fully aware that His pur

without the synergy of gene____,

"all the generations".

ACKNOWLEDGMENTS

First of all I want to thank my lovely wife of 50 years who has forever stood by my side and was always faithful to encourage me along the journey….including the writing of this manual. I also want to thank my church family (Northland Harvest Church) and the Leadership for releasing me to devote time and energy into this project. Bruce Iverson (Teacher) is part of the Leadership Team at Northland and was willing to avail his grace gifting to write Chapter five on "Church Government" (thank you Bruce). Also, a special thanks to Rebecca Armstrong who made her cabin (with a beautiful lake side view) available for some "alone time" to finish the project. I also want to thank the Leadership Team of Ascension Fellowships International (Dan Semsch, Rich Conley & Phil Cruz) for affirming and encouraging me on this journey. And a special thanks to Pastor Kevin Barsotti (Havre, Mt.) and Vickie Hieb (family friend from Hudson, MN) for their wisdom, grace and patience in serving me with their editing skills. And of course our own children.. Jarrod, Shantal, Troy & Mark who weathered the storms of life with us, staying the course and discovering their own destiny. Most of all…."thank you Jesus for making yourself known to me in 1971"..an experience that forever changed my life!

CONTENTS

THE MASTER PLAN: BUILT TO LAST!

Introduction!

There is probably nothing that stirs my heart more than conversations regarding the purpose of mankind here on earth and what God has destined for His people. I believe it would be fair to say that most of us have failed to realize that "destiny" is more than just something down the road (future). Our past and our present have destiny written all over them (Ephesians 1:4; Psalms 139:16). Having said that, I am fully aware there are a number of components involved in finishing the course and finishing well. Fulfilling our destiny is something very dear and close to the heart of the Father. So much that He gave His only begotten Son to pave the way for us to experience His best. As we come to understand the past, present and future of our destiny, it will have a profound effect on how we live our lives. We will also discover our destiny is bigger than us. It involves a people who understand the ways of God and are willing to align themselves with Him "the author and finisher of our faith" (Hebrews 12:2).

At the moment I am being reminded of a couple of scriptures of which one of them addresses the "times" we are living in and is found in Hebrews 12:25-29. Please keep in mind all scripture references in this study are taken from the New King James Version (NKJV) unless otherwise specified. The author of Hebrews is making it very clear that God is speaking today and strongly admonishes us to not "refuse Him who speaks" (Heb.12:25). Verse 26 says "He has promised, saying, 'Yet once more I shake not only earth, but also heaven'. Now this 'Yet once more' indicates the removal of those things that are being shaken, as of things that are made, that the things which cannot be shaken may remain. Therefore, since we are receiving a kingdom which cannot be shaken, let us have grace, by which we may serve God acceptably with reverence and godly fear". Two things are very evident in this scripture, (1) we are living in a time of great shaking, and (2) that which will not be shaken is of His kingdom. Without question the nations (including our own) are being shaken (earthquakes, floods, fires, political systems, educational systems, media, families, etc.). However, in the midst of all that is being shaken there is that which still remains, His Kingdom!

This leads me to the second scripture which is found in the gospel of Matthew 7:24-27. We find Jesus bringing His famous "Sermon on the Mount" (Kingdom living) to a conclusion and is challenging His listeners with these words, "Therefore whoever hears these sayings of Mine, and does them, I will liken him to a wise man who built his house on the rock: and the rain descended, the floods came, and the winds blew and beat on that house; and it did not fall, for it was founded on the Rock." Conversely, the opposite is true, "Now everyone who hears these sayings of Mine, and does not do them, will be like a foolish man who built his house on the sand: and the rain descended, the floods came, and the winds blew and beat on that house, and it fell. And great was its fall." As we can see from these few verses in Matthew, *everyone* heard the "sayings" but not everyone did them. And the winds of adversity, the floods, the rains, etc., beat on both houses and yet only one remained, the one that was built upon a solid foundation, the Rock Himself (Jesus Christ). How the Church is being built is critical to seeing reformation and city transformation. We must give attention to not only the foundation but also how we build on it. Paul, the apostle, writes these words in I Corinthians 3:10, "According to the grace of God which was given to me, as a wise master builder I have laid the foundation, and another builds on it. But let each one take heed how he builds on it". You will find the next five verses to be very challenging!

As I meditate on these few scriptures, it becomes very clear to me that God has designed His House is to stand the test of times. Both houses are full of eternal destiny and purpose. However, the house that stands is the one that will have a profound effect upon cities, states and nations being transformed. I have therefore chosen to entitle this book, "The Master Plan: Built to Last".

God has spoken very clearly to me that after 33 years of pastoring it is time to put on paper some of the things I have learned in building a Kingdom work that's designed to last! And because there is "no end to the increase of His government (Kingdom) and peace" (Isaiah 9:7), I continue on the journey, forever learning that His ways are higher than mine (Isaiah. 55:9). The Church at large and the Kingdom of God are very dear to my heart (and His) and whenever I refer to them it will be with a capital "C" and a capital "K" in contrast to the local church and other kingdoms. My desire is that this will be a "lasting work" (a handbook per se) to assist the generations in bringing forth reformation and transformation to cities and nations.

Chapter 1

THE IMPORTANCE OF A KINGDOM PERSPECTIVE

One of the greatest mistakes Christians make is that we define the Kingdom of heaven (or God) as someplace we go after we die. Yet, as we shall see in His word, there is so much more to His Kingdom that is relevant to our lives being lived out here on earth today. The subject of the Kingdom of God has no boundaries. A few pages in this book will not do justice to the vastness of its influence here on earth. And I am not one who believes everything will be a utopia before Christ returns. I do believe, however, we (the Church) can make a profound difference in many cities and regions as we come into alignment with Him and His will while waiting for His return.

Jesus made it very clear (Luke 19:13) that we are to occupy (verb, not a noun) until He returns. At this appointed time the "fullness" of His Kingdom reign will take place here on earth. In the meantime we have the privilege of preparing the way for His soon return and coming Kingdom.

Scripture makes it very clear that we will never have a Kingdom perspective without a revelation of the King Himself (Jesus). Jesus presented His disciples with a very important question, a question that all of mankind must face in (Matthew 16:15-19) "Who do you say I am?" As Peter discovered, the right answer could only come by revelation from the Father through the Holy Spirit. However, upon this revelation of "who He is…the Christ the Son of the Living God", He is going to build His Church and the gates of hell will not prevail.

These three things we must never forget:

(1) It is His Church (not ours/mine)…

(2) He is building it (not I), and…

(3) The gates of hell will not prevail against it.

His discourse did not stop there but proceeds with the promise "And, I will give you the keys of the Kingdom of heaven, and whatever you bind on earth will be bound in heaven, and whatever you loose on earth will be loosed in heaven". He has given to the Church the "keys of the Kingdom" and the authority to use them. Once again I beg to ask the question.."can we (the Church) make a difference?" That is certainly His intent!

Why is this message of the gospel of the Kingdom of God so important? This was Jesus' main message throughout His lifetime and even after His resurrection.

John the Baptist introduces the message of the Kingdom as he prepares the way for this coming King in Matthew 3:1-2 stating "Repent, for the Kingdom of heaven is at hand!"

As Jesus steps into His earthly ministry (Matthew 4:12,17,23), we find Him sharing the same message of the Kingdom with signs following "healing all kinds of sickness and all kinds of disease among the people". Wow! What a powerful message and truly "good news" to the world!

You will discover His message never changed throughout His earthly ministry, nor did the signs stop following the message (Matthew 4:24; Luke 4:40-44 and all of Matthew 13). I would encourage you to take time to do a word study on the Kingdom of God. It will revolutionize your thinking as it is such a profound subject. So profound that Jesus even spent His last 40 days on earth, after His resurrection "speaking of the things pertaining to the Kingdom of God" (Acts 1:3). Knowing He would be departing soon, He wanted to make sure they received and understood the "main message", the gospel of the Kingdom of God!

This precious message, the gospel of the Kingdom of God, continued on in the book of Acts (8:12). Here we find Deacon Philip preaching "things concerning the Kingdom of God and the name of Jesus Christ, both men and women were baptized". There were obvious signs and miracles being done which even caused Simon to believe (8:13). Simon's heart was not right as he wanted to buy the power which was not for sale (and never will be)! We then find Paul the apostle at Ephesus (Acts 19:8) preaching in the synagogue for three months, "reasoning and persuading concerning the things of the Kingdom of God". The result of Paul's obedience to preach the Gospel of the Kingdom was "unusual miracles" (verse 11) and the "word of the Lord grew mightily and prevailed" (verse 20).

As Paul comes to the end of his life (Acts 28:30-31), he is still found "preaching the Kingdom of God and teaching the things which concern the Lord Jesus Christ with all confidence". No wonder Jesus taught His disciples to pray "Thy Kingdom come, Thy will be done on earth as it is in heaven" (Matthew. 6:10)!

So what about this Gospel of the Kingdom? How do I experience it and why is it so important? I will endeavor to answer these questions based on His Word. Jesus said (John. 3:3), "unless one is born again, he cannot see the Kingdom of God". In verse five He expounds further by making the statement, "unless one is born of water and the Spirit, he cannot enter the Kingdom of God".

The first requirement is that you "must be born again" in order to see the Kingdom. If you have never surrendered your heart to Christ (the One who died for your sins), I encourage you to do so now because He wants to have a relationship with you. His love goes much deeper than a "casual relationship". He wants you to get to know Him. Do not be satisfied by "watching" the Kingdom from afar. Instead "enter" into the freedom the Kingdom has to offer. Ask the Holy Spirit to reveal to you the love of God through His Son, Jesus Christ, and by faith invite Him to take up residence in your heart. The Holy Spirit will be faithful to reveal to you the "unsearchable riches of Christ"(Ephesians 3:16-19).

Ezekiel 47:1-12 is a prophetic picture of what we are talking about. Don't be satisfied with an "ankle deep" relationship with Him. Jump in the river where you can't touch bottom. Learn to swim with Him and enjoy the ride! Remember, wherever the river goes it brings life and healing (verse 9)! This is the Kingdom of God!

1. What is the nature of the Kingdom of God? In I Corinthians. 4:20, Paul writes.. "For the Kingdom of God is not in word but in power". This again confirms the power and authority behind the Gospel of the Kingdom of God. It is not mere words!

In Romans 14:17, Paul writes, "for the Kingdom of God is not food and drink, but righteousness and peace and joy in the Holy Spirit". Did you get that? His Kingdom is a Kingdom of righteousness, peace and joy. In these last days the Church should be full of these three ingredients!

2. When is the Kingdom of God? For this answer we turn to the Author Himself (Jesus) who in Mark 1:15, who states "The time is fulfilled, and the Kingdom of God is at hand. Repent (change your minds/belief system) and believe in the Gospel". Again Jesus makes this statement in Matthew 12:28, "But if I cast out demons by the Spirit of God, surely the Kingdom of God has come upon you". On the basis of scripture there is no other conclusion we can come to other than NOW is the time of His Kingdom.

3. Where is the Kingdom of God? Here is what the King had to say in Luke 17:20,21, "Now when He was asked by the Pharisees when the Kingdom of God would come, He answered them and said, The Kingdom of God does not come with observation; nor will they say, 'See here!' or 'See there!' For indeed, the Kingdom of God is within you." Wow! The Pharisees had the same question that many of us have today. The answer has not changed! The Kingdom is within us! Paul writes these words in II Corinthians. 4:7, "we have this treasure in earthen vessels that the excellence of the power may be of God and not of us"! His plan from the very beginning was to use clay vessels like you and I. Humbling and liberating at the same time.

4. The last question regarding the Kingdom of God is, "what is the future of the Kingdom of God?" I addressed the answer to this question in my "Introduction" and encourage you to read it again. His Kingdom is unshakeable and eternal (Hebrews 12:28). When Isaiah prophesied (9:6,7) about the coming King some 750 years before His arrival, he wanted to make sure we understood that of the increase of His government and peace there would be no end! We can and should be experiencing His Kingdom today in an ever increasing way.

How we view the Kingdom and how we understand it will have a profound effect on what we say, what we think, the songs we sing, the prayers we pray, how we live, how we respond and how we build. The "keys" have been given to us; blueprints have been approved, the permit has been granted. It is time to build!

Chapter 2

OLD TESTAMENT BLUEPRINT

I begin this chapter by drawing our attention to the book of Acts and its reference to the "congregation" (Church) in the wilderness. This reference is in regards to the Children of Israel and their journey to the Promised Land under the leadership of Pastor Moses. Acts 7:37 says, "This is that Moses, who said to the Children of Israel, The Lord your God will raise up for you a prophet like me from your brethren. Him you shall hear" and vs. 38, "This is he who was in the congregation in the wilderness... and with our fathers, the one who received the living oracles to give to us". The "prophet" that Moses made reference to in verse 37 was none other than Jesus Christ!

Further in the chapter (verse 44), Luke addresses the tabernacle of witness in the wilderness and how Moses received specific instructions (blueprints) on how to build it. It is not my intent to do an in-depth study on the Tabernacle of Moses, however, you will find it to be a very fascinating study. The author of the book of Hebrews makes it clear that the Tabernacle of Moses "serves as a copy and shadow of the heavenly things, as Moses was divinely instructed" (Hebrews 8:5). In this study, you will discover all things point to Jesus and the building of the true tabernacle which the Lord erected, not man (verse 2). This study will also enlarge your understanding of the New Covenant!

Let us go back to the Old Testament to see what God had in mind. In Exodus 25:1-9, we find the Lord instructing Moses to speak to the

7

Children of Israel to bring offerings of certain items for the building of the tabernacle. The only requirement was that they bring their offering "willingly"! I find this quite fascinating, realizing the offering had no value unless the heart was willing! Verse 8 states "And let them make Me a sanctuary that I may dwell among them". This sanctuary was not just any old sanctuary, but one designed in heaven. God had shown Moses the specific "pattern" while he was on the mountain, and continued to remind Moses to build accordingly until the tabernacle was completed (Exodus 25:40, 26:30, 27:8). He makes it very clear (29:42-46) to Moses that the tabernacle represents His presence in their midst and that He is coming to meet with them. The tabernacle will be sanctified (set apart) by His glory!

As we come to the end of the book of Exodus (40:33-38), we find these words "So Moses finished the work"! Because he built it according to the pattern shown him on the mountain, a "cloud covered the tabernacle of meeting, and the glory of the Lord filled the tabernacle". Can you imagine the glory of God being so heavy in the tabernacle that Moses was unable to enter it? Wow! This Glory cloud led them, kept them warm, and protected them throughout all their journeys.

Thinking about the Glory cloud leads me to ask two questions:

1. Just as there was a pattern (blueprint) for building the Tabernacle of Moses, the Church in the wilderness, is there also a pattern (blueprint) for the New Testament Church?

2. And if that is true and we build according to the blueprint, will He fill His house with His glory?

I am convinced that the answer to both these questions is affirmative and relevant to every generation until Jesus returns to earth! Let us go to His Word and discover the real thing (not a shadow), never forgetting that the "Glory of the latter house will be greater than the former" (Haggai 2:9).

Chapter 3

NEW TESTAMENT BLUEPRINT

In the last chapter we discovered there was a pattern that Moses was instructed to follow for the building of the Tabernacle for the church in the wilderness. Moses' obedience in following the blueprint resulted in God filling the tabernacle with His glory. This became His dwelling place amongst His people. I therefore proposed to you two questions: 1) Is there a pattern revealed in the New Testament on how to build His Church? 2) If so, and we follow the blueprints, will the end result be His Glory once again filling the temple?

In this chapter and chapters following, we will endeavor to answer these questions. First, I want to address Jesus' last words before He ascended into heaven (Matthew 28:18-20) better known to us as "The Great Commission". I quote the Master Himself, "All authority has been given to Me in heaven and earth. Go therefore and make disciples of all nations, baptizing them in the name of the Father and of the Son and of the Holy Spirit, teaching them to observe all things that I have commanded you; and lo, I am with you always, even to the end of the age".

Mark, in his Gospel records the same account only in a more detailed manner (Mark 16:15-18). "Go into all the world and preach the gospel (the Kingdom) to every creature. He who believes and is baptized will be saved; but he who does not believe will be condemned." Then He adds "And these signs will follow those who believe. In My name they will cast out demons, speak with new tongues, if they take up serpents or drink anything deadly it will not harm them, they will lay hands on the sick, and they will recover".   Jesus was making it very clear that the goal was not just new converts but disciples who would present the Gospel of the Kingdom to nations in word and deed. He would confirm the good news with signs following! Jesus had in mind nations and gave authority, grace and anointing to the Church to accomplish the task. Therefore, it is fair to conclude that how we build the house is critical to the assignment He has given us. It must be built to last!   Let's begin by examining the foundation.

Paul's epistle to the Ephesian Church is without question one of the key books in the Bible for gaining insight as to how the Church is to be built. In Ephesians 2:19-22, Paul writes these words, "Now therefore, you are no longer strangers and foreigners, but fellow citizens with the saints and members of the household of God, having been built on the foundation of the apostles and prophets, Jesus Christ Himself being the chief cornerstone, in whom the whole building, being joined together, grows into a holy temple in the Lord, in whom you also are being built together for a habitation of God in the Spirit".

Paul makes it clear that apostles and prophets are essential for the foundation; keeping in mind there is only one cornerstone (Jesus Himself). He is saying that upon this foundation the Body of Christ (His Church) is being built for a habitation (dwelling place) of God. Remember that the tabernacle of Moses was a shadow of things to come. In Moses' Tabernacle, God dwelt amongst them; but in the temple (tabernacle) He is building today, He is dwelling inside us! Glory!

As we proceed to Ephesians chapter 4, we find Paul expounding further on the revelation he received regarding the Church and how it is to be built. Verse 10 proclaims "He who descended is also the One who ascended (speaking of Christ) far above all the heavens that He might fill (pervade) all things". The word pervade means "to become diffused throughout every part" (Webster dictionary). Jesus ascended into the heavens that He might be diffused throughout His Body (Church). Verse 11 states "And He Himself gave some to be apostles, some prophets, some evangelists, and some pastors and teachers". We will refer to these gifts as the five-fold ministry. He gave these gifts (verse 12) "for the equipping of the saints, for the work of the ministry, for the edifying (building up) of the Body of Christ, till we all come to the unity of the faith and the knowledge of the Son of God, to a perfect (mature) man, to the measure of the stature of the fullness of Christ". The Greek word for "perfect" is *teleios*, which means complete, mature, full age, growth of mental and moral character. Let's take some time to examine these few verses.

Paul makes it very clear that these five-fold ministries were given to the Church, not to do all the work, but to equip the Church for the work of ministry. Jesus would call this "making disciples"! And as the Church (not the pastor) would do the work of the ministry, there would be a building up of the Body of Christ. Not only would the Body be built up, it would literally take on the life, character and nature of Christ Himself (a mature expression of Him here on earth).

Over the years the Church has had no problem accepting the ministry of the pastor, the evangelist, and the teacher. However, embracing the ministry of the apostle and prophet has not been an easy transition for the Church at large. There are two basic reasons for this:

1. We have been told (and believe) that the apostolic ministry ceased when the last of the twelve apostles died.
2. Secondly, we have chosen to remain ignorant on the subject because it doesn't fit in with our theology. I want to take some time here to share my own personal testimony on this subject.

Nine years after I committed my life to Christ, God began to speak to me about Ephesians 4:11 and the five-fold ministry. The year was 1980. I had been at a Bible camp in northern North Dakota (Lake Metigoshe), and was casually walking by a book table when it suddenly folded up and all the books fell to the floor. As I reached down to assist the lady managing the book table, my eyes fell on a particular book that I had not heard of and the Holy Spirit spoke very gently to me saying "you must buy this book"! Immediately, I picked up the book and said to the lady, "How much is this book? I must buy it".

I finished helping her and headed to my room to begin reading the book titled "The Body of Christ..a Reality" by Watchman Nee. That book revolutionized my life starting me on a journey that continues today. First of all, it opened my understanding to the fact that God's heart has always been for a people (a Body known as the Church) who would be that Kingdom influence here on earth. I learned that the five-fold ministry was essential to equip the Body for such a task. I must confess that up to that point I had had very little hope for the Church. Most of my experiences had been fear, unbelief, church splits, doctrinal differences, strife, division, and the list goes on! However, the book of

Ephesians took on a life of its own and I began to see past the frailty of man (including myself). I transferred my confidence to the Head of the Church; none other than Christ Himself!

At the time this was being revealed to me, I was serving as an elder in an independent church and the pastor had granted me the privilege to teach an adult Sunday school class as well as doing some pulpit ministry. I did this with his blessing and encouragement or so I thought! However, as I journeyed down the road "expounding" on the reality and function of the five-fold ministry, I began to detect some resistance (such as the pastor not speaking to me for six weeks).

Freedom was granted to talk about pastors, evangelists and teachers, but apostles and prophets were off limits for fear of these offices being a cult. However, this belief created a problem as I could not deny what God had already shown me. In my youthfulness I tried to make others see what I saw to little or no avail. The result of my actions was my family's departure without a lot of fanfare. As scriptures say, "how can two walk together unless they agree?" This leads to the question, "where do we go from here?"

Chapter 4

HOW THEN SHALL WE BUILD?

At this point I was faced with a dilemma: how do I move forward without a group of people? Much to my "surprise", I wasn't the only one God was speaking to during this season. A core group of people were beginning to get a glimpse of the Kingdom of God and what God wanted to do in and through the Church. In 1982 we linked arms and became known as Shiloh Christian Fellowship in Minot, North Dakota. We became part of an apostolic movement known as Ascension Fellowships International (AFI), whose head office was located in Pueblo, Colorado. AFI served as a spiritual covering to us. God was moving across our nation and several apostolic networks of churches were being raised up. How refreshing and comforting it was to discover we were not alone, and most of all not crazy!

Now we could begin the task of imparting Kingdom understanding and establishing apostolic order to a willing people (Shiloh Fellowship). One of the elders who served with me in my pastoral role was Bruce Iverson, a man with a vision for the Kingdom of God and apt to teach. What a blessing and source of encouragement Bruce has been and remains today as a respected and gifted teacher in our midst. Bruce has graciously accepted the task of writing the next chapter concerning the role of elders in the local church.

The first item on our agenda was to teach on Divine order (five-fold ministry) and the role these ministries perform in bringing forth and establishing His Kingdom here on earth. Ephesians chapter 4, verse 14 states "that we should no longer be children, tossed to and fro and carried about with every wind of doctrine, by the trickery of men, in the cunning craftiness by which they lie in wait to deceive, but , speaking the truth in love, may grow up in all things into Him who is the head, Christ, from whom the whole body, joined and knit together by what every joint supplies, according to the effective working by which every part does its share, causes growth of the body for the edifying of itself in love". Jesus ascended and gave these five-fold gifts so we would no longer be tossed to and fro by every wind of doctrine, and that the Body might "grow up" into Him where every part is doing its share causing great growth. So, what does that look like?

The rest of this chapter is devoted to gaining an understanding of how these various ministries function and what they bring to the Body. Please keep in mind that Christ is the perfect example of the Apostle, the Prophet, the Evangelist, the Pastor and the Teacher! He was the ultimate expression of all five-fold ministries. And the more connected these five-fold gifts are to the Head, the more His nature will be displayed through them. Ministers are clay vessels but still gifts to the Church. To the best of our ability, let's endeavor to keep our focus on the ministry gift and not on the title. I will be referring to the gifts as "apostolic grace", "prophetic grace"...etc. My objective is to address some of the characteristics of these individual grace gifts that have been given to the Church to be expressed through "clay vessels". As in all gifts, the effectiveness of the gift is in proportion to the character of Christ being formed within the clay vessel. My intent is not to make this an exhaustive study on Ephesians 4:11, however, I would encourage you to become a faithful Berean (Acts 17:11) and "seek out the scriptures to see whether these things be true or not". The first gift we will address is the apostle.

APOSTOLIC GRACE

Let's begin by bringing some clarity to the apostolic grace and its function in equipping the Church for ministry. We have already learned that the apostolic grace is one of the foundational ministries (Ephesians 2:20) and plays a vital role in making sure the Church stays focused and in alignment with the Chief Corner Stone (the Rock, Christ Jesus!). This grace gift is representative of "Christ the Apostle" (the Sent One) who came to earth to redeem mankind back to the Father, and is therefore "one sent on a mission" (Webster Dictionary). Keeping this role in mind let's take a look at some of the main attributes of this gift:

(1) Sees the big picture: True apostolic grace has an understanding of the role of the Church (Ekklesia) in these last days and what will be required of Her. The "making disciples of all nations" (including our cities, communities, states and regions), will require the involvement of the Church (Body of Christ), not just a local congregation, which is no small task.

(2) A passion to see His character formed in each believer: Paul the apostle was acutely aware that the transformation of families, cities, states, regions and nations could not

17

happen apart from His character being displayed through a people, and he was willing to travail (as in labor) until Christ be formed in the Church at Galatia (Galatians 4:19).

(3) <u>Intent on making known the "hidden mysteries" of Christ</u>: Paul made this clear in his letter to the Church at Colosse (Colossians 1:24-29). He understood the importance of the Church obtaining a revelation of the mystery of "Christ in you, the hope of glory". Paul was fully convinced there would be no glory or "growing up" in the Church apart from the Church receiving a revelation of the power and authority of the Christ within them.

(4) <u>They are "treasure hunters"</u>: Apostolic grace has an uncanny ability to discern the "treasure" in the earthen vessel. Just like the men who came to David when he was hiding from King Saul in the cave of Adullam (I Samuel 22:2), men " who were in distress, in debt and discontented" became mighty men of war under the leadership of David. Many times these are the "no names, no face" people. Knowing every person has purpose and destiny here on earth causes us to look more at what is inside the cup rather than only view the outside.

(5) <u>Called to be fathers</u>: Paul writes to the Corinthians (I Corinthians 4:15) reminding them they "might have 10,000 instructors in Christ, yet do not have many fathers". There is such a need for "fathers" (and mothers) in this hour due to the fatherless generation in our midst. I have also discovered there are many sons who want to be fathered

and daughters who want to be mothered. In many circles we are literally experiencing the fulfillment of Malachi's prophecy, (Malachi 4:5-6), where the hearts of the fathers are turning towards the children and the hearts of children are turning towards the fathers. Oh God, restore the family unit once again!

PROPHETIC GRACE

We must not forget that the prophetic grace is also one of the foundational ministries listed in Ephesians 2:20, and must purpose to work together with the apostolic grace in order to make sure we are building upon the Rock Christ Jesus. This particular grace gift is representative of "Christ the Prophet". Luke reminds us of the words that Moses spoke to the fathers in Acts 3:22,23, "The Lord your God will raise up for you a Prophet like me from the brethren, Him you shall hear in all things, whatever He says to you. And it shall come to pass that every soul who will not hear that Prophet shall be utterly destroyed from among the people". After feeding the 5,000, John writes (John 6:14), "Then those men, when they had seen the sign that Jesus did, said, this is truly the Prophet who is come into the world". Listening to and then obeying His voice is a serious matter! Let's take time here to address four of the attributes of this grace gift to the Church:

(1) Prophetic grace has a passion for the Church to be hearing the now word that God is speaking to the Church at large as well as to each local assembly. As we examine the seven

19

churches in the book of Revelation (Rev. 2 &3), we discover there was a different message for each church and each church was challenged in this manner, "He who has an ear, let him hear what the Spirit says to the churches". The inference here is that it is possible to hear, but not hear!

(2) This grace gifting not only carries a burden for the "word" to be heard, but also for the word to be released and obeyed. As we read in Genesis 1, nothing happened without it first being spoken. Heaven is moved when the "now word of the Lord" is released upon the land.

(3) The release of prophetic grace is necessary to help keep the Church on track by giving it direction. Jesus spoke these words in Matthew 10:41, "He who receives a prophet in the name of a prophet shall receive a prophet's reward". He goes on further in the same verse applying the same principle to a righteous man. It is quite evident this principle applies to all five ministry gifts listed in Ephesians 4:11.

(4) Passion to see God's Glory in His house is a large part of their lives. It can only happen as God's people embrace and obey the now word of the Lord! Their passion is to see the Church come into alignment with the Head (the Word). They have great need of apostolic grace to help administrate this passion.

EVANGELISTIC GRACE

Now that the foundations have been laid, let us move on to begin the building process. The question is, "What do we have to build with?" This is where the Evangelistic grace comes in knowing that it is the Lord's will "that none should perish but that all should come to repentance" (II Peter 3:9). Through the preaching of the Gospel of the Kingdom, the "burnt stones" (Nehemiah 4:2) are turned into "living stones" (I Peter 2:5) to be used in building a spiritual house and a holy priesthood. Once again, Jesus is the perfect example of the evangelistic grace, having given His own life that others may live! In fact the wisdom, love, and grace He demonstrated with the "woman at the well" (John 4) is a perfect example of this gifting. Let us now examine some of the attributes of this precious gift to the Church:

(1) It is obviously no secret that the passion that drives this grace gift is none other than seeing souls come to Christ. They can't help but preach the Gospel knowing that "whoever calls upon the name of the Lord shall be saved. How then can they call on Him in whom they have not believed? And how shall they believe in Him of whom they have not heard? And how shall they hear without a preacher?"

(2) They have no fear in sharing Christ and seem to have a keen awareness of those in their midst who do not know Christ as their personal Savior!

(3) Because of this strong desire to see souls come to Christ, they often overlook the need for personal discipleship and

can often become impatient with the other four gifts given to the Church.

PASTORAL GRACE

The obvious fruit of the evangelistic grace in the Church is souls coming to know Christ. They come as "babes in the Lord" needing special attention and love. Their presence can often disrupt life as usual. The pastoral grace comes in to help lead, feed, nurture, and protect the flock. This is no small task as it is much like having a new baby in the home needing special care (feeding, diapers changed, etc.). The Church over the centuries has had little problem accepting the role of the pastor, the evangelist, and the teacher. However, accepting and understanding the role and responsibilities of the apostolic and prophetic grace has been a different matter. At the time we began this journey of "building to last", the word apostle was deemed cultish. I am happy to report that as the Church has moved forward, a shift has taken place (and still continues), in accepting and embracing apostolic/prophetic grace in the church. Keep in mind that the Chief Shepherd (Pastor) of all times is none other than Jesus Christ Himself. Pastoral grace attributes include:

(1) Their first passion and concern is for the well- being of the flock God has entrusted into their care.

(2) Because of their mercy motivation, they are driven to do everything they can to protect, heal and nurture (feed) the flock in their care.

22

(3) Relationships within the Body are very important to them as they know and understand that sheep are in great danger when they wander away by themselves.

(4) Because of healthy and proper relationships (including unconditional love), they have the grace and ability to "speak the truth in love".

TEACHER GRACE

This grace gifting is essential in helping the Body "grow up" so it can fulfill its destiny and purpose here on earth. It's one thing for people to get saved (evangelistic grace) and cared for (pastoral grace), but quite another for them to learn how to stand and walk in their respective callings (teacher grace). This cannot happen apart from a proper diet of the word of God and a relationship with the Holy Spirit. Let's take a few moments to examine the attributes of this special gift to the Body of Christ, knowing that Jesus Himself was the greatest Teacher that ever walked this planet. He has now taken a part of this grace and deposited it in clay vessels.

(1) The obvious passion for teachers is that the word of God is being taught and preached. This is not the "letter of the law" but the life of the "living word"! Their heart is for each believer to be aware of the "promise of entering His rest" (Hebrews 4:1) and that no one come short of it. This cannot happen without the word of God as it "is living and powerful, and sharper than any two-edged sword, piercing even to the division of soul and spirit, and of joints and marrow, and is a discerner of the thoughts and intents of

the heart" (Hebrews 4:11,12). Applying the word is a must for one to become an overcomer and cease from his own works. Then he can enter into His rest!

(2) Their heart is not just for each believer to know the word, but to know the "living word". Believers will never know who they are in Christ and who Christ is in them without knowing the living word. He is the truth. Only knowing the truth will set us free (John 8:32).

(3) Teachers have the awesome responsibility of unlocking the unsearchable riches of Christ that Paul makes reference to in Ephesians 3:8. Helping the Church discover the width, the length, the depth, and the height of Who He is and His love for mankind (Ephesians 1:16-19)! He is the living Word and in Him we live and move and have our being (Acts 17:28).

(4) Teacher grace is set in our midst to assist in unfolding and building on the foundations that have been laid by apostolic and prophetic grace.

As you can see by now, all of these grace ministries are necessary to equip the Church so it can fulfill its assignment here on earth. The Church is being transformed into the fullness and stature of Christ. This is what He intended before the foundations of the world! If one or more of these grace gifting are lacking or not embraced, the Church will become anemic and never reach its potential. In the next chapter we will be discussing the need and place of elders in the local church and the vital role they play in helping the Church fulfill its destiny for both individuals and the Body of believers.

Chapter 5

CHURCH GOVERNMENT

(By Bruce Iverson)

One of the questions often asked today is: "What is the proper form of government in the New Testament church?" Many of us have grown up in various forms of church government and carry with us a great diversity of ideas.

Jesus said new wine must be put into new wine skins. In examining church government and what God desires to impart to us, it is important that we do not allow tradition to impede what God is doing today. A careful and prayerful examination of the Scripture, God's wisdom, and a humble heart are all necessary to discover truth.

THE RULE OF THE ELDERS IN THE LOCAL CHURCH

In the New Testament we have a number of scriptures that clearly tell us that elders served as the governmental body of the local church. Paul wrote in **1 Timothy 5:17** "let the elders (*presbuteros*) that rule (*proisteemi*) well be considered worthy of double honor, especially those who work hard at preaching and teaching."

Peter also gives responsibility to the elders in **1 Peter 5:1-2** when he exhorts the elders to "...shepherd (*poimaino*) the flock of God among you, exercising oversight (*episkopeo*) not under compulsion, but voluntarily, according to the will of God..."

Paul, in exhorting the elders of Ephesus in **Acts 20:28** warned, "Be on guard for yourselves and for all the flock among which the Holy Spirit has made you overseers, to shepherd the Church of God which he purchased with his own blood." In **I Thessalonians 5:12**, Paul encouraged the Thessalonian believers to "...appreciate those who diligently labor among you and have charge (*proisteemi*) over you in the Lord and give you instruction."

There also exists evidence that is inferred throughout the New Testament that elders were appointed in every local church, after the church had become established in order to bring order and stability to church life. Paul's missionary trips and Paul's Epistles evidence this truth.

Later we will examine the Greek words to help us gain more insight into eldership and the function of an elder. The qualifications of eldership found in Timothy and Titus are well-known. However, the actual outworking of eldership is not that well documented. One can conclude from their title, and on the basis of scripture, that elders were in charge of the overall care and direction of the church.

Elders were overseers of local churches. To understand the function of an elder, one must first understand government. Government is defined in the dictionary as "to exercise authority over, direct, control, rule or manage".

In the local church, elders were given authority to oversee those whom God had joined to the church. Passages drawn from various parts of the New Testament reveal that in the early church, elders were expected to exercise authority, not only in spiritual matters, but also in direct domestic matters and other aspects of life that had a direct influence on the church. **Acts 20:28; Romans 12:8; 1Thessalonians 5:12; 1 Timothy 3; and 1 Timothy 5:17.**

The goals of government worked to ensure that the church followed the doctrines of the Lord Jesus and the apostles; that proper order was maintained in the church and the home; and that the needs of the church, both spiritually and physically, were being met. It was important that there were no divisions within the body and that conditions were such that the church could grow in numbers while remaining at peace with one another and with the community around them.

If we examine the paragraphs above and then compare the early church elders with modern-day elderships, not only in denominational churches but also in independent and charismatic bodies, we see how far we have strayed from the practice of the early apostolic Church. There are many reasons why this is true. It is vital for the church to ask, "Is it God's desire to restore the full function of the eldership within the local church, and if He does, what changes are needed to facilitate this restoration?"

I firmly belief it is the desire of God to restore the function of the eldership within the local church. Though we do not have all the understanding that is necessary at this time, we are moving in the right direction. As God continues to restore truth and revelation comes to the church, all facets of this area of church life will be restored.

EXAMINING THE GREEK

The Greek word most often used in the New Testament for elders is *presbuteros*. It is used 67 times in the New Testament and comes from the root *presbus* which is translated "elderly". Another important word is *episkopos* which is translated "Bishop". It is used five times in the New Testament. In **Acts 20:28** this word is translated as "overseer". *Episkopeo* is the verb form of "bishop" and is translated "looking obligingly; taking oversight".

The noun for pastor (*poimen*) is found only once in the New Testament in **Ephesians 4:11**. The verb "to pastor" (*poimanio*) is the word translated "to shepherd", and is always used to express the function of elders.

From the original Greek, we understand the elders were older, not necessarily by age but by experience. They were more mature Christians who were given authority and oversight over the church. They were to shepherd God's church, which according to Jesus' admonition to Peter in **John 21:15-17** and Peter's subsequent plea to the elders in **1 Peter 5:1-2,** was to "feed the sheep" and "to tend, direct and exercise authority". The context of **1 Peter 5:1–3** makes it clear that proper shepherding involves walking before (leading) the sheep and setting the right example for them to follow.

The qualifications for eldership are given in **1 Timothy 3** and **Titus 1**. As one examines these qualifications, it should be noted that they revolve mainly around the moral character of the individual. Maturity is the key in eldership.

In **Acts 14:21–28**, we see Paul and Barnabas returning to the churches that had been established. "… they returned to Lystra, Iconium, and Antioch, strengthening the souls… and when they appointed elders for them in every church, having prayed with fasting, they commended them to the Lord in whom they had believed." No doubt these men were of high reputation within the church. They had proven themselves through moral excellence and faith that they could carry this responsibility.

Paul's farewell to the elders of Ephesus in **Acts 20:17 – 38,** gives weight to the great responsibility the apostle was leaving with the elders as he departed. It is easy for us to understand why God's first priority for the government of his church was moral character. God was entrusting His church to men who could be depended upon.

From the pattern we see in the New Testament, elders were appointed through apostolic and prophetic ministry. Paul in his admonition to **Titus** in **1:5** said, "for this reason I left you in Crete, that you might set in order what remains, and appoint elders in every city as I directed you…" Eldership was seen as critical in the life of the church and the church was not complete until the eldership was in place.

ELDERS AND ASCENSION MINISTRIES

Ascension ministries (when Christ "ascended" He gave) listed in **Ephesians 4:11** and eldership are not necessarily one in the same. One may have an ascension gift yet not be an elder within the local church. Later we will discuss the question if all elders possess an ascension gift.

As we noted in the qualifications for eldership, which are quite explicit, greater importance is placed on the moral character of the individual. The elder's behavior, how he portrays himself outwardly, how he relates to his wife, his family and the community, are the conditions by which he is to be judged.

In eldership God desires individuals of established character and moral excellence to govern His church. Paul makes it very clear that being an elder is not an option for a new convert (**I Timothy 3:6).**

These truths reveal the dynamic of the church in the New Testament. The church was a living, dynamic organism after Jesus' resurrection. It was filled with a spiritual presence that was truly spectacular. Both Paul and Peter make reference to the church being a spiritual house "filled with the presence of God." We see in Paul's writings that spiritual "happenings" were the norm and the spectacular was commonplace. Each individual Christian was a conduit for the Spirit of God. Consequently, all were expected to add to the life of the church.

As new converts were added, these truths of the indwelling Spirit, the power of God, and individual function were taught to each believer. As believers took their place within the church, the dynamic of the body continued and grew. Medically, an organism that grows without control is called a tumor. When there is controlled growth within a body, organs develop and mature. As the early church grew, the need for order became more amplified, not for the purpose of restraining His Church, but providing a safe environment for the Church to fulfill its purpose and destiny.

Elders did not provide the growth of the church. The Spirit caused the growth. Elders were there to ensure that growth. The dynamic of the body as well as the function of the body was orderly and based upon the truths and foundations laid down by the Lord Jesus, the apostles, and the prophets. The important characteristics of elders were strength of character, moral integrity, and a mature relationship with Christ.

As stated earlier, ascension ministry is a gift of Jesus based upon the call of God. Unlike eldership, there is no prohibition against young men functioning in gift ministry. We have all witnessed individuals who moved powerfully in ascension anointing and yet were found to be morally flawed at a later date. Moral integrity and personal holiness are essential in all ministry. However, it is important to understand that the power of ascension ministry and the gift of an ascension calling comes from God and is not based on man's education, talent, or age.

Nowhere in Scripture can I find a list of qualifications for ascension ministries. One cannot qualify for a grace gift. However, that does not imply that gift ministry has no standard. Individuals who flow in gift ministry are measured by the highest standard, that of Christ's ministry. As James wrote in **James 3:1**, "Let not many of you become teachers, my brethren, knowing that as such we shall incur stricter judgment." We can assume that all gift ministry falls under the same canopy of God's judgment.

ARE ALL ELDERS PASTORS?

As stated earlier, the word for pastor (*poimen*) is found only once in the New Testament in **Ephesians 4:11**. The verb form (*poimaino*) is used in **Acts 10:28** and **1 Peter 5:2** when speaking directly to elders of the church and their responsibility to the church.

There are questions as to whether all elders are *poimen* by calling. Certainly all ministry grows in stature and there will be young elders who will mature in their ministry as there will likewise be developing apostles and prophets in the body of believers.

One of the problems in answering this question is the view churches have of the responsibility of the pastor. In many traditional and contemporary churches, the pastor is called to minister to all the needs of the church. Most of these individuals are anointed by God in one of the gift ministries. They have answered the call of God within their spirit and received anointing from God to fulfill their call.

However, when they arrive at their churches, they are expected to pastor, teach, evangelize, be business managers, and perform a thousand other duties. Of course, most fail in those areas that they are not called or anointed for service. When this occurs, the congregation deems them a failure and releases them.

The verb "to pastor" is *poimanio* and is translated "to shepherd". When Jesus commissioned Peter in **John 21:15-17** to shepherd His lambs and sheep, His commission involved the use of two verbs. In verse 15 and 17 the verb *bosko* is used, which is translated "to provide food, to nourish, to feed." In verse 28, *poimaino* is used meaning "to feed sheep, to tend sheep."

We can conclude that pastoral ministry is shepherding, which involves feeding and tending. Nowhere is it implied in Scripture that the responsibility of the entire church's needs falls to the pastoral ministry. This idea evolved with the introduction of the "professional clergy" and is not scripturally sound. The consequence of this has left churches impotent in body function and led to multiple ministries being shipwrecked on the rock of false expectations.

Eldership is shepherding, but the role of the elder is more clearly defined in Scripture as relating to government. Pastoral ministry, according to **Ephesians. 4:11-12**, is a gift given to the church by the ascended Christ and is given for "equipping the church for the work of service." We can conclude that the ministry of elder and pastor, although they may touch in areas, are distinct.

THE PLURALITY OF ELDERS

In all instances in Scripture where elders were mentioned as having governmental authority, they were mentioned in the plural. Plurality of eldership was the norm of the New Testament church. Study of New Testament eldership leads us to believe that elders were appointed in plurality, functioned as a plurality and were the government of the local church. There has been much discussion about this, but there is no direct evidence that there was a head elder or chief elder. There were just elders **(Acts 15, 20:7; Titus 1:5, 1Peter 5:1).**

Although elders are appointed in plurality, all elders are not the same. Elders are not co-equal in their calling, gifting or experience. In a church there will be young elders. There will be elders who have ascension giftings **(Ephesians 4:11)**. There will be elders who are wise and mature. Each elder and his gifting is taken into account by the eldership when decisions are made.

Elders have governmental anointing upon their lives and are charged with the overall health and welfare of the church. Elders function as a group (team). Elders are equal in their governmental responsibility making governmental decisions as an eldership (plural). Each elder is unique and has strengths and weaknesses. No single elder has greater governmental authority within the eldership.

ELDERS WITH MULTIPLE MINISTRIES

Often in church government, those who are elders will also function in one of the five-fold ministries **(Ephesians 4:11)**. This is not always the case and there will be elders who function only governmentally in the local church.

Learning to function as an eldership in plurality is not a simple task. Eldering is learned over time and through experience. Elders who are gifted in ascension ministries lean toward the strengths of their callings. Apostolic elders will desire to lead the church outwardly. Prophetic elders feel the local church needs to hear a fresh word from God. Teaching elders see the needs of the church in terms of more teaching. Pastoral elders sense the needs of the body in terms of meeting their felt needs. Elders who are gifted evangelists desire to see the body out witnessing and winning souls for the Lord.

As one can see, it is necessary for these strengths to be brought into balance under the direction of the Holy Spirit. Elders need to function as a unit. The needs of the church are diverse. It requires sensitivity and mutual submission from each elder to assure that the church is moving in God's direction.

Functioning together is something that is a learned experience. When one is anointed for government or ministry or both, he must understand that maturity does not occur overnight. As in any spiritual endeavor, there are lessons to be learned and maturity to be gained by doing, experiencing, failing and enjoying success.

It is of critical importance that each elder understands that he shares equal responsibility with the rest of the eldership. Decisions are to be made in plurality and the church must embrace the truth that God has deposited within the eldership governmental anointing. If the body is to be balanced, the elders must function as an eldership. The eldership is responsible for the overall health of the body, the overall direction, and the spiritual life of the church.

All ministry within the local church is subject to the eldership. If there are apostles, prophets, or other ministries within the local church, their authority does not supersede that of the elders.

As stated earlier, each ascension gift has a sphere of authority and should be respected and embraced by the eldership. When decisions are to be made concerning a need or direction within the local church, those individuals who carry the burden of that particular ministry should be given greater preference. If there are teaching needs within the church, it is normal to look to "teachers" to give direction and aid. If the church is wounded or hurting, the pastoral gifts need to be given liberty to fulfill their ministry call.

At various times and seasons more emphasis will be placed on a particular gift ministry within the body to meet the needs of the church.

Young churches need pastoring and teaching. More mature bodies should be functioning in apostolic, prophetic and evangelistic ministry. As the church becomes mature, all the ministries should be flowing together, building one another up and producing life in the church and community.

THE ROLE OF SENIOR MINISTRIES

All ministry grows in grace and maturity. Within churches there will be individuals set apart by God and recognized by the eldership as senior ministries. Usually these individuals occupy the senior pastor role, even though their gifting may be in other ascension callings. Senior ministries do not have more authority in governmental decisions than the other elders. However because of the grace upon them, they bring liberty and wisdom to the eldership.

Senior ministries are important for many reasons. One key benefit is in the area of administration. When elderships meet, senior ministries keep the eldership informed as to the financial condition of the church, the spiritual state of the church, and other various needs the church may be encountering. The senior minister can act as a chairman for the eldership to the church and as a spokesman for the church to the community.

Some elderships fear recognizing senior ministries, as they believe this is giving one member more authority. This is not the case. Mutual submission and trust within the eldership as well as the understanding that the burden of government falls upon all the elders releases ministries to function to their fullest capabilities.

Shared governmental responsibility within the eldership also benefits senior ministries by releasing them to function in the areas in which they are gifted. No longer is the senior pastor expected to meet the diverse needs of the church but he is given release to flow within his gift calling.

Another great benefit of recognizing senior ministry coupled with shared governmental responsibility is that it promotes diversity of ministry within the church. Since one man is not in charge or expected to meet all the needs, young and diverse ministries are encouraged and promoted within the body.

The goal of the eldership and ascension ministries within the church is to see the body "grow up in all aspects into Him, who is the head, even Christ." **Ephesians 4:15**. All ministry should be servanthood in nature.

THE HEAD ELDER CONCEPT

As stated earlier, there is no evidence in early New Testament churches of a head elder. Much has been written about this subject by sincere individuals but the truth remains that nowhere in Scripture is this ministry identified.

Often man has sought to combine the things of God with the things of man. Many of man's institutions work well for their intended purposes. Often we believe that cloaking God's church in these garments will bring the same results. Unfortunately, we have witnessed in our church structures the folly of this practice. Problems often arise within the church if one elder or ministry is recognized as having more authority than the other elders. Whatever ministry anointing is upon that particular individual will become the emphasis of the church. The "overall" health of the body will not be met. We see this throughout Christianity where we have "faith churches", "holiness churches", prophetic churches", etc.

Usually these movements have started from an individual who has a powerful anointing in his or her particular gifting. A church is formed where all other ministries are subject to the "emphasis" ministry. At first, these churches flourish because God is blessing the anointing that rests upon the individual. However after a period of time, if the ministry does not come into balance the church suffers and stumbles and often ceases to exist. The emphasis ministry cannot meet all the needs of the church.

In "emphasis" churches there is often a high turnover in the congregation as the flock seeks ministry in the areas that are lacking. The church can end up being populated by believers who have the same gifting or ministry as the original founder. Instead of becoming a dynamic living organism, it becomes stunted, ineffective and unbalanced in ministry.

Another area of concern in "head elder" government is the lack of accountability. There are many churches that have been torn asunder because the senior man was accountable to no one. They have fallen into error, sin or simply taken the church in a direction not intended by God and would not receive correction because of the belief that they alone were the head of the church.

Plurality of elders and shared governmental responsibility brings accountability and balance to the local church. It also brings great freedom in ministry.

It is important to understand there are many wonderful churches that have been founded by single individuals and emphasis ministries. There are also many churches that do not have a perfect governmental structure but are fulfilling God's intended purpose here on earth.

GROWING ELDERSHIPS

In Paul's missionary journeys he would spend many months laying the foundations of the gospel. In examining passages in the book of Acts, phrases such as "house to house", "day and night", and "anything that was profitable", give us insight to the great passion Paul had for the church.

Romans 12:1; 1 Corinthians 12 and Ephesians 4 give us a taste of the teaching and revelation that Paul brought concerning the church. His great desire was to see churches grow up into all aspects in Christ. It is interesting that in the Book of Revelation Jesus addressed His admonitions to churches and not to individuals.

In **Titus 1:5** Paul wrote "For this reason I left you in Crete that you might set in order what remains, and appoint elders in every city as I directed you…" The eldership in Paul's understanding and revelation was a key element in the life and future of the church.

Today God is setting His church in order. Plurality of elders, the role of ascension ministries, the government of the local church, etc. are truths the Lord is revealing throughout the body of Christ.

Effective elderships do not occur overnight. They require time and effort. As with all spiritual endeavors there will be struggles and adjustments. As we embrace the truths the Spirit is revealing many blessings will come.

I hope this information has been of help to you. If you are interested in these truths we invite you to contact us. As a church we are seeking God's best and look forward to seeing the church of Jesus Christ grow into all that God has intended.

Some personal thoughts concerning: "The Role of Women in the Church"

(By Larry Borud)

As I approach this subject I am very much aware there are numerous positions concerning the role of women in the church. And in no way is this meant to be an exhaustive study on this subject matter. I personally take a very strong position that the "Church will not fulfill its designed purpose" without acknowledging and embracing the role of women in the Church. These are my personal convictions and not necessarily in alignment with everyone I relate to. I must confess that women (including my wife) have played a very important role on my journey of discovering and fulfilling my Kingdom assignment. And I believe that is what God had in mind from the very beginning.

I will, therefore, approach this subject from a Kingdom perspective that is presented to us in the first chapter of Genesis (1:26-28). "Then God said, 'let Us make man in Our image, according to Our likeness; let *them* have dominion over the fish of the sea, over the birds of the air, and over every creeping that that creeps on the earth'. So God created man in His own image; in the image of God He created him; male and *female* He created them. Then God blessed them, and God said to them, 'Be fruitful and multiply; fill the earth and subdue it; have dominion over the fish of the sea, over the birds of the air, and over every living thing that moves on the earth."

The Creator of the universe makes it clear from the very beginning that mankind has a major role to play in bringing and maintaining order over His creation. He therefore created man in His image (male and female) giving them specific instructions to "be fruitful and multiply; fill the earth and subdue it; and have dominion…" over everything He created. Wow..what a powerful assignment! In other words the assignment given to mankind <u>could not</u> be accomplished without man (or woman).

I find it interesting that when it comes to His purpose for mankind here on earth, He makes no distinction between male and female. He makes it very clear that both genders are necessary for the establishing of His Kingdom. In the New Testament we find Paul confirming this truth (Galatians 4:26-29) stating that we "are all sons of God through faith in Christ Jesus" and that "there is neither Jew nor Greek, there is neither slave nor free, there is neither *male* nor *female;* for you are *all* one in Christ Jesus."

Then again in Matthew 16:16-19, we find Jesus assuring Peter that upon the revelation of who He was, He would be building His Church and the gates of hell would not prevail. Even handing over to them (male and female) the "keys of the Kingdom" for binding and loosing. That together, they could fulfill their assignment in bringing heaven to earth (Matthew 6:10).

Is it possible we have made "gender" the issue instead of the grace gifting in each individual (male or female)? We cannot deny that scriptures teach (I Corinthians 11) that the head of woman is man and that woman is to submit herself to her husband as unto the Lord (Ephesians 5:22,23). However, the part we seem to forget is that "husbands are to love their wives as Christ loved the Church"…so much He gave Himself for her. What would happen if all husbands received the grace of God (they can't do it on their own) to live out this principle? I am convinced if husbands could love and lead like Christ, there would be many women drawn and released into their Kingdom destiny. The world (and the Church) have yet to experience what it will be like when men begin to "lead" with a Christ like nature…loving their wives as Christ loved the Church…laying down their lives for this prize possession. The Kingdom mandate in Genesis 1:28 still stands for all generations and genders…."be fruitful, multiply, fill and subdue the earth..and have dominion over His Creation." It will never happen without male and female!

Maybe we need to give some thought to a quote from Carol McLeod (author and popular speaker): "The husband is the head of the home but the woman is the heart. So, which would you rather live without….your head or your heart?!" The question concerning "the role of women in ministry" is one that all local Leadership are having to face. May God grant us wisdom and understanding of the Father's heart concerning this very important issue.

Chapter 6

THE MASTER'S PLAN

In this chapter we will address the danger of focusing on only one of the five-fold ministries listed in Ephesians 4:11. All five-fold ministries are necessary to assist the Body of Christ to become what God has purposed it to be and to remain Christ centered. The Body is to be equipped to do the work of ministry and to be so conformed to His image that we talk, act, and live like Him manifesting His nature and character here on earth (Ephesians 4:13). Anytime one or more of these equipping ministries are ignored or over emphasized, the Body will be weakened. As we learned from Bruce's teaching in the last chapter, plurality and diversity are near to the heart of God and Who He is (Father, Son, and Holy Spirit). We are going to address these five equipping ministries one by one and see what happens when there is no relationship (or desire to relate) with any of the other four grace giftings, therefore becoming an island unto themselves. Let us begin with the Teacher gift.

Teacher-Emphasis

Let's take a few moments to review the strengths (chapter 4) of the Teacher grace gifting in our midst. As you recall, their passion is for the "word". Their heart is for every individual to know the word as well as the "living Word" that they might discover (a) who they are in Christ and (b) who Christ is in them. This grace gift has been given to the Church by Christ to help each of us to become grounded in Him, the solid Rock, so that when the storms of life come upon us we will not be moved. You may ask, "What danger is there in this?" We must never forget that His purpose is for us to be Christ centered. When we become anything other than that, we slip into error. This means that if all we are hearing (or being taught) is just "word, word, word" (we call this being *word_centered*), it can easily lead to legalism! So instead of ministering "life" it begins to minister death. Relationships suffer, whether they be with other people (family, friends, parents, children etc.) or our relationship with our Heavenly Father, creating a consciousness of sin_rather than a consciousness of righteousness (Romans 10:1-3 and Hebrews 10:1-3). Please understand that being "word centered" is not wrong, but very incomplete if room has not been made for the other four equipping ministries. In fact, you will see at the end of this chapter the importance and bountiful fruit of these five ministries working together, which I have subtitled the "Synergy of the Ages"! We will now address the danger of only a "pastor mindset".

Pastor-Emphasis

As we learned in chapter four, the main strength and passion of a pastoral gift is the genuine care and concern for the flock. Where the Teacher would create a "word center", the pastoral grace creates a *"care center"*. Once again, a vital part of the whole but in and of itself without balance will eventually lead to self-centeredness. Instead of speaking the truth in love, everything becomes permissible so that we do not offend anyone thereby creating a breeding ground for lawlessness. Pleasing people takes priority over pleasing Him. At this level there is very little tolerance and time for the other four ministries resulting in a very in-grown body of believers with no vision beyond the local church. What about the Evangelist?

Evangelist-Emphasis

Once again, the strength and passion of this five-fold ministry is to see souls come to Christ. This is a worthy vision! We call this the *"lost centered"* church where all the resources and energy go towards their love for the mission field and desire to see people saved. There is great value placed upon relationships outside the church. "People" are potential candidates for salvation. Once again, all this is very dear to the Father and the main reason He sent His Son to earth (to redeem mankind). So what's wrong with just being a lost centered church?

Generally speaking, these churches are very weak when it comes to the word due to the emphasis being predominantly on getting people saved (salvation messages not just outside but within as well). The result of this is usually limited revelation and understanding of the Kingdom of God with most (if not all) resources going towards evangelism. In most cases it is the "leader's vision" and not necessarily the Body's. Most leaders who are zealous for the lost have a difficult time fitting into the "pastoral mold" resulting in little tolerance and patience to pastor needy people. Once again, a very legitimate gift that left to itself can cause more harm than good. So what about the prophetic grace?

Prophetic-Emphasis

As we know, this ascension gift puts great emphasis on "hearing and obeying" what God is saying. Obedience is a strong word in their vocabulary as they place great emphasis on the "now word" of the hour or season of the Church. Their heart is for people to get connected with the "proceeding word" that is coming from heaven and for the release of that particular word over the land, cities, states, nations, families, etc. They also carry a burden for God's people to know how to operate in the gifts of the Spirit (I Corinthians 12, Romans 12) with prophetic understanding of the times we are living in so we might know what to do and how to pray (I Chronicles 12:32). There is a call in their bones for "justice" and righteous judgments. So what's wrong with a vision such as this? This is this not the heart of the Father?

As with all the other gifts, in and of themselves there is nothing wrong other than they can't go this road alone! Churches with only a prophetic propensity often become "mystical" having no practical outworking or expression! The prophetic word drives the bus. These churches are known as *"Revelation Centered churches"*. You will normally find that the leaders of these expressions will become very impatient with the "nuts and bolts" of normal church life. Because of this prophetic bend, it is very easy for them to become black and white, with a resounding REPENT! This, of course, leads once again to legalism, bringing forth death instead of life. So what about the apostolic grace? How could this particular grace gifting get out of balance? Let's take a moment to examine the dangers of only apostolic grace.

49

Apostolic-Emphasis

As you recall, apostolic grace is focused on the "big picture" and reaching the finish line (*Vison Centered*)! There is an uncanny awareness within them to search out the "hidden treasures" within common people that are necessary to accomplish the task that is before them. These are fields (people) that have been overlooked, passed over, ignored or often forgotten (Matthew 13:44). This brings dignity and value to individuals who had no understanding of destiny and God's purpose for their lives, and now see themselves involved in His eternal purposes (Ephesians 3:9-11). Where they once walked in shame and condemnation, they now walk with their heads held high in the love and forgiveness of the Father, able to take their rightful position in the army of God. The fact that the vision is "bigger than us" inspires them to reach beyond their man made boundaries embracing the wider Body of Christ. What could ever go wrong with this?? Let's look a little closer!

By its very nature, the "big picture" concept causes these people to be "far-sighted" where the goals and visions become the driving force in reaching the finished product. Therefore, without the balance of the other four ministries, it will gravitate towards being "my" vision instead of "His" vision. Those who "get in the way" of my vision will likely get stepped on. Once it moves into "my vison", mercy goes out the window and we begin to "pick and choose" those who can help fulfill "my" vision. Instead of accountability partners, we embrace, train, and select "yes men" who will serve me! We find ourselves relating only to those who can help us fulfill our vision. What more need I say! So let's get a bird's eye view of what this might look like when all five- fold ministries are working together.

Synergy of the Ages

What do we mean when we use the word "synergy"? Webster defines it as: "where the effect of the combined parts working together is greater than the sum of the individual parts". For example, one horse can pull a wagon with six ton of hay while two horses working together can pull thirty two tons! Think of the force (synergy) that can be released when these five-fold ministries are working together for the sake of equipping the Church for its eternal purpose. What could stop such a force? What we learned (as an apostolic network) over the seasons was that we must shift from "five-fold ministry" to a "five-fold people" (Ephesians 4:11-13). In order to fulfill our mission, we grow into His fullness and stature. Without making the shift we will find ourselves in a maintenance mode of putting out fires, rather than igniting the fires of His eternal purpose.

As the five-fold ministry works together to equip and prepare God's people for ministry, there will be a demand placed upon the individual anointings within the Body of Christ. They will no longer be "tossed to and fro and carried about with every wind of doctrine" (Ephesians 4:14). They will find themselves relating to one another resulting in a "growing up in all things into Him who is the Head" (Ephesians 4:15,16). The end result will be a stable, relational, unified, and functional Body of Christ becoming a fulfillment of the Master's prayer in John 17:20-23. The world is waiting! The earth is groaning! So what does an apostolic people look like as we are making this shift from an individual five-fold ministry to a corporate five-fold people (the synergy of the ages)?

Apostolic-People

This Body of believers called the Church (ekklesia) is becoming apostolic in nature. Believers are beginning to see the big picture and becoming aware they have been called to the Kingdom for such a time as this (Esther 4:14) to bring reformation to cities, businesses, schools, homes, etc. right where they live. They are fully aware that the task before them is "bigger than them" and will require a people (better yet an army) who are sold out to the eternal purposes of God. They also realize that residing within each person (even the unborn) there is a "treasure" (anointing) that is meant for God's eternal purpose. They become "treasure hunters" bringing hope to the hopeless and dignity and value to each person. They find themselves aligning with Paul's apostolic prayers in Ephesians, Philippians, and Colossians. Their prayers and intercessions are shifting from prayers of petition to prayers of decrees, thus releasing His Word over the land.

Prophetic-People

Not only is the Church becoming apostolic in nature, but it is also becoming prophetic. Because the Church is beginning to see the big picture, there is great need to hear what God is saying and see what

God is doing now. Jesus was the perfect example of this principle (John 5:19, 30). Their heart is to not only hear what God is saying, but to obey and release His Word over the land. Because of the demand being placed upon them, they are beginning to understand it is not by might nor by power, but by His Spirit says the Lord (Zechariah. 4:6). A growing awareness of our need for His anointing and the gifts of the Spirit are essential in bringing forth reformation. Can you sense the spiritual synergy building?

Evangelistic-People

With the fire of the apostolic and prophetic burning in the bones of His Church, vision for the lost is taking a different perspective. We no longer want them to just get saved to go to heaven. We want them to get saved because we need them and each one is filled with eternal purpose since before the foundation of the world. Now this necessitates "getting into the world" but not becoming a part of the world, which is a very fine line. We will not discover the "treasures" by standing on the outside looking in and judging them. With apostolic and prophetic eyes we see them not just lost, but full of eternal purpose. This brings a whole new dimension to evangelism and the reason why the evangelist is necessary to equip the Body for evangelism.

Teacher (Word)-People

Even the teaching ministry takes on a whole new dimension. Now we have "saved people" with apostolic and prophetic grace in their bones who need to be taught the word. Apostolic and prophetic foundations need to be laid in these individual lives. The need to come into a relationship with the "living Word" is essential in acquiring the freedom promised in Him (John 8:32). As the "word" comes alive in His people they are diligent to share it with others (in word and deed) that they might know the importance of who He is in us and who we are in Him. We are beginning to understand that His Word is the final authority on all things. There are truly unsearchable riches of Christ waiting to be unlocked and revealed to those who seek after Him (Ephesians 3:8-11).

Pastoral-People

Now we have an apostolic people with world vision with a heart longing to hear the "now word" of the Lord in order to fulfill the Masters mandate to "go forth and make disciples of all nations" (Matthew 28:18-20). The fire of evangelism is burning within them knowing His will is that "none should perish but have everlasting life" so they can fulfill their Kingdom destiny and purpose here on earth. These people not only need to be saved and taught, but now they need to be pastored. They need to be loved on, nurtured, and ministered to so they can become whole and finish their journey here on earth.

This is a perfect picture of "synergy"! The church (His Bride) is becoming an *Apostolic center* where people see the big picture and realize they have been commissioned to earth and have need of one another. She becomes a *Prophetic center* where people are rich with the Living Word and desperate to know what He is saying and doing. Plus an *Evangelistic center* where people are intent on reaching the lost to bring them into the Kingdom, and a *Teaching center* where people teach others how to have a living relationship with the Word. The synergy of the Church culminates as a *Pastoral center* where people rise up and minister to the needs of mankind. This, my friend, is the most powerful force upon the earth! He is building His Church and the gates of hell will not prevail!

As we come into alignment with Him, we are going to witness not only a synergistic anointing upon the five-fold ministry, but also upon (1) the generations, (2) plurality of elders, (3) the Body of Christ, (4) husbands and wives, (5) male and female ministry, (6) kings (leaders in the marketplace) and priests (leaders in the Church), and last but not least, (7) a synergy of creativity. As Kingdom leaders, we have a responsibility to provide an environment that is conducive to releasing "creativity" upon the land. This will require a shift (change) in our emphasis and how we think with the end result being "a people of influence", which we will address in the next chapter.

Chapter 7

A PEOPLE OF INFLUENCE

In the last chapter we discussed the transition the Church is going through in becoming an apostolic people with a Kingdom vision. A people who are desperate to know and hear what God is saying. A people who understand the lost condition of mankind and their need for a Savior. A people who hunger for God's Word to be taught so lives will be transformed. A people who are rising up to care and minister to the needs of mankind becoming people of great influence here on earth.

Suddenly the Great Commission (Matthew 28:18-20) takes on a whole new meaning. Where once "missions" was someplace far away, it has now become next door, my city, where I work, etc. We call these the "Mountains of Influence", a concept that was birthed out of the heart of Bill Bright and Loren Cunningham (a story in itself).

The specific mountains (places of influence) they identified are (1) Religion, (2) Family, (3) Education, (4) Media, (5) Arts/Entertainment, (6) Government and (7) Business. Invariably, every person is involved in one or more of these mountains and has been called and anointed to make a difference. We call this "city transformation" which will require a change in the way we think about missions and church life.

Up to this point, most of church life has taken place within the four walls of the church building and has become a structure (often lifeless and irrelevant) instead of a living organism full of life. In order to become "people of influence" in these mountains, there will need to be a shift in our thinking and how we do church. God continues to remind us through His word that the "Church" is not a building where we meet but a people who have a relationship with one another and with the Head of the Church (Jesus Christ). That being said, let me offer seven suggestions as a starting point to assist you in this transition. These are not exhaustive in and of themselves and can be tweaked to fit your specific situation.

1. *From an individual mindset to a corporate mindset*: As we learned in the previous chapter, what God wants to do (and is about to do) will require the "wider Body of Christ". It is much bigger than one individual church and demands from us a "reaching over" to my brothers and sisters from other denominations. This is what we would call the "Church in the city"! I have discovered over the years that the Body of Christ in the city finds it easier to make the transition than its pastors and leaders. It demands from us a shift in our thinking from building my church to building His Church. As pastors, we must become very intentional in availing ourselves for this transition. Ezekiel 47 paints a vivid picture of what this can look like, a stream becoming a river, so deep you have to swim! Verse nine promises "And it shall be that every living thing that moves, wherever the river goes, will live. There will be a very great multitude of fish (harvest), because these waters go there; for they will be healed, and everything will live wherever the river goes."

Now that describes the Church in the mountains of influence (whatever mountain)!

2. *From "The King is coming" to "His Kingdom is coming"*: This one may raise a few red flags for a couple of reasons. To some it may challenge their eschatology which is not my intention. I believe we can all agree that the "King is coming back" even though we don't know when. However, He has instructed us to "occupy" or do business (Luke 19:13) until He returns. He also instructed His disciples to pray "thy Kingdom come, thy will be done on earth as it is in heaven". This says to me that while we are here on this earth (or until He comes) we can be actively involved in bringing His Kingdom to earth (like the mountains of influence) fulfilling the "doing business" mandate. I must go on record stating my own personal conviction that I do not (nor do I believe scripture teaches) that everything is going to be a utopia when Christ returns. However, I do believe that as we (the Church) come into alignment with Him and His ways, our Kingdom influence can bring Kingdom transformation to cities and geographical areas. Jesus Himself promised (John 14:12) that with the help of the Holy Spirit (which was to come), we would do the works He did and even "greater works than these he will do"! What opportunity avails us as we come into alignment with Him and His ways resulting in a people of great influence.

3. *From "retirement" thinking to "generational" thinking*: This thought can also rub people the wrong way. Obviously, as men (and women) get older (70 myself), we discover some of the physical things we used to do we can't do anymore or at best we do at a "much slower" pace. Having said that, it is not time to "check out" but to check in. The need for "fathers and mothers" is very great. We are witnessing the last verse of the Old Testament (Malachi 4:6) being fulfilled before our very eyes. The hearts of fathers are turning towards the children and the hearts of the children are turning towards their fathers. We now have the privilege of ministering to a "fatherless generation". Let us not forget that our assignment here on earth as the Church cannot be accomplished apart from the generations working together. Joel prophesies of a time (Joel 2:28) in history where God will pour out His Spirit on all flesh (we are living in that time) and "your sons and your daughters shall prophesy, your old men shall dream dreams, your young men shall see visions". I call this the "experience vs. creativity" principle and it does not happen without some healthy tension. Probably the greatest test of this principle happens in the arena of music ministry! I can personally testify there is grace to bring the generations together and as fathers/mothers it is not a matter of handing the baton to them but "learning" how to run with them (of course at a slower pace). Let there be a redeeming of the years that the locusts have eaten (Joel 2:25)!

4. *From organizational to organic*: What does this mean? God created us to be "relational" (Genesis 1:28). We must realize that "organization" in and of itself does not necessarily bring life. Yet Paul admonishes us (I Corinthians 14:40), "Let all things be done decently and in order". So the question remains, where is the balance in all of this? Let us not forget that the Holy Spirit is a gentleman and where the Spirit of the Lord is there is liberty (II Corinthians 3:17). I continue to find myself on a learning curve regarding this matter. I am discovering there are times when order brings bondage (choking the life out) and there are other times when order brings great liberty. I have personally discovered that the greatest enemy of true liberty is religion, and I don't mean having a personal relationship with Jesus Christ. Religion says "it has to be my way" or "we have never done it this way before" leaving no room for others to express themselves (or be creative) without making them feel condemned or "less than". I have also discovered that when things happen "organically", they take on their own order. As we see in scripture, Jesus Himself had to constantly contend with the religious Pharisees. He did so by never doing the same thing the same way, like healing the sick, etc. Yet He raised up twelve men who turned the world upside down! Wow!

5. *From a "positional" mindset to a "grace gifting" mindset:*
Paul the apostle addresses this issue in his letter to the
Corinthians (I Corinthians 12:1-11) by admonishing us in the
first verse that we are not to be ignorant concerning
spiritual gifts. This means it is possible to be ignorant. He
continues by reminding us in the next few verses that there
are "diversities of gifts, differences of ministries, and
diversities of activities" (verses 4-6) but the same Spirit, the
same Lord, and the same God who works in us all. As each
person functions in his or her grace gifting it will profit all.
This is a strong confirmation of what we learned in chapter
four regarding the five-fold ministry equipping the Body for
the work of ministry where each part is doing its share
(Ephesians 4:11,16). It is certainly fair to say that we make
the mistake of elevating people into "positions" where they
do not have the grace for it and end up being square pegs in
round holes, finding themselves highly frustrated,
unfulfilled, condemned, and most certainly, not enjoying
what they are doing. Whenever we function "outside" our
grace gifting, we automatically do what needs to be done in
our own strength and ability rather than His grace. The
Church must become more diligent in helping the Saints
discover their "sweet spot" so they can be trained and
released into their destiny. This requires healthy, strong,
secure leadership that understands the principle and is not
threatened by God's ways. Honoring this principle brings
great freedom to people to do what God has called them to

do and not feel condemned because of other's expectations (including their own).

6. *From a pastoral model to an apostolic model*: We will spend a little more time explaining the difference between these two models in the next chapter. However, I must go on record making it very clear that I am not "anti-pastor" as this might infer. In fact, I share a very strong conviction of the need for pastors and a pastoral people in the days we are living in. But I am also aware (as we learned earlier) that pastoral grace has a very difficult time seeing the big picture and vision is usually localized within the four walls of the church. The reason for this is because of their legitimate care and concern for the local flock and God's plan for each individual to be plugged into a local church. This is certainly not bad, but without the complementary grace of apostolic vision the tendency is to stay within the safety and security of the four walls! This of course will prevent them from fulfilling their God-given destiny and purpose in life. It is not uncommon for there to be great contention and strivings within as everyone endeavors to protect their turf and the playing field gets full or in many cases, the pastor does it all. And if it falls only on the shoulder of the pastor, he will end up doing much of the work in his own strength and not under the anointing of the Holy Spirit. Without making this shift it is easy to become very self-centered and protective of "my church"!

7. *From "world" culture changers to "Church" culture changers*: May we never forget the Master's words in John 3:16,17, "For God so loved the world that He gave His only begotten Son, that whoever believes in Him should not perish but have everlasting life. For God did not send His Son into the world to condemn the world, but that the world through Him might be saved". In other words, God has placed His people here on earth and has empowered them to make a difference (and, yes, even change the culture). The point that I want to make is that we have great faith in the world changing our culture through fear, ignorance, intimidation, etc. In fact, we have seen it happen in a literal sense right before our eyes. While the Church was sleeping the enemy came in and sowed weeds in our midst (Matthew 13:24-30). Most of the time we didn't even know the difference between the good seed and the bad seed. Jesus said, "let them grow together until the harvest" (verse 30) which is the hour we are living in. We (the Church) must believe that just as the world can change the culture, so can the Church. Reformation can really happen on our watch as "greater is He that is in us than he that is in the world"! But it cannot happen when the Church is locked inside the four walls and has no vision or hope that things can be different. The "seven mountains" of religion, family, education, media, arts and entertainment, as well as government and the business world are waiting for Kingdom people to be raised

up to bring Kingdom influence. This will result in cities, states and nations being transformed. We (the Church) have been called to the Kingdom for such a time as this (Esther 4:14) to change times and seasons. All of creation is waiting for the manifestation of the sons of God (Romans 8:19). We have been called to "make a difference" because of the Christ living within us.

Chapter 8

CHURCH MODEL VS. KINGDOM MODEL

After much prayer (and some consternation) I have decided to add this chapter to the book. Once again I must add a disclaimer that just as I am not "anti-pastor", neither am I "anti-church". In fact, it is just the opposite. I am extremely pro church knowing it is the vehicle that God has chosen to make a difference on this earth. The heart of this chapter has come about through the experiences of serving in a pastoral role for 33 years. Much (if not all) of what I have written in the previous chapters has come from my experiences in almost 50 years of church life. As with all of life, there have been glorious seasons and there have been difficult ones. Through them all, I have purposed to keep my heart pure, knowing I could not lose if I did so. I must confess there was one time when my wife reminded me of the "great loss" (which there was). But because of His redemptive nature and faithfulness, He has restored to me the "years that the locust have eaten" (Joel 2:25), and might I add, much more than I lost!

Please refer to the previous chapters before reading this one. The earlier chapters will give understanding to what you are about to read. The scripture basis for this chapter is taken from the Old Testament (Micah 4:1-2 & 6-10). The first two verses state, "Now it shall come to pass in the latter days (of which we are living in) that the mountain of the Lord's house shall be established on the top of the mountains, and shall be exalted above the hills; and peoples shall flow to it. Many nations shall come and say, 'come and let us go up to the mountain of the Lord, to the house of the God of Jacob; He will teach us His ways, and we shall walk in His paths,' for out of Zion (the Church) the law shall go forth, and the word of the Lord from Jerusalem".

It is obvious from this scripture that the Mountain of the Lord will overshadow all the other mountains. Knowing it is possible (because I have been there) to believe in the Church without any understanding of the Kingdom has prompted me to write this chapter. For the Church to fulfill its assignment here on earth, it must have an understanding and perspective of the Kingdom of God (please read chapter 1 again). In addressing these two mindsets, I have come up with 12 areas that I believe will help change the way you think about the church and the role of the Kingdom in church life. Let's examine the difference between the two: *Church Model vs. Kingdom Model*

1. *VISION*: Pastor driven vison vs. Elder (plural) led vision

    What you believe concerning the Kingdom will have a profound effect on your vision. If the people have no vision of the Kingdom, then by default the pastor is not only responsible for the vision, he has to "drive" the vision. This means everyone has to come into alignment with his vision. However, an elder led vision leaves room for each person to pursue and discover their own "sweet spot" and the mountain God has called them to inhabit. At the same time they will continue to be covered, led, protected and nurtured by a plurality (team) of elders. There is safety and wisdom in the multitude of counsel.

2. *MESSAGE:* Gospel of salvation vs. gospel of the Kingdom

This can also be a very sensitive subject as it would appear that the good news of salvation is not important, which could be no further from the truth. However, I know it is possible to preach the message of salvation without any understanding or revelation of the Kingdom which often results in making the two messages the same. I also know that you cannot preach a pure message of the Kingdom without including salvation. They do go hand in hand, but are not the same. Intertwined in the message of the Kingdom is a Church legislating (occupying) here on earth until Jesus returns. Conversely the message of salvation leans more towards the "closing out" of the church age and escaping the great tribulation. Regardless of how you view the end times, we have been instructed by the Master Himself to occupy until He comes.

3. *PERSPECTIVE:* Build a church vs. build the Church

Kingdom people carry a vision for the city, state, region, and nation(s). They know that in order for reformation to take place it will take a village (the Church). Therefore, they become very intentional in relating to the wider Body of Christ and the community, making way for these things to take place. Without a vision for the Kingdom and its influence in your city, all your energy and time will go into building your church. That is not what God had in mind as He has called the Church to create a culture of honor by respecting and embracing one another. And they sang a new song, saying, "You are worthy to take the scroll, and to open its seals; For You were slain and have redeemed us to God by Your blood out of every tribe and tongue and people and nation, and have made us kings and priests to our God; and we shall reign on the earth" (Revelation 5:9-10).

4. *FOCUS*: Getting right with God vs. the treasure within.

We must not minimize the importance of "getting right" with God. In fact, we learned in chapter one that you can't even "see" the Kingdom without being born again. Becoming a "new creation in Christ" (II Corinthians 5:17) is the first step towards fulfilling your Kingdom destiny. Paul reminds us (II Cor. 4:6-7) that "it is God who commanded light to shine out of darkness who has shone in our hearts to give the light of the knowledge of the glory of God in the face of Jesus Christ. But we have this treasure in earthen vessels that the excellence of the power may be of God and not of us". We, the Church, have failed to recognize (or understand) that salvation takes place from the inside out. Paul further instructs us to "work out your own salvation with fear and trembling; for it is God who works in you both to will and to do for His good pleasure" (Philippians 2:12-13).

Let us not forget that when Jesus raised Lazarus (John 11:44) from the dead and brought life to him, He said to those around him, "loose him and let him go". Even though Lazarus had been raised from the dead (salvation) he was still bound hand and foot with "grave clothes".

Instead of ministering guilt and condemnation to those who are "still bound", let us recognize that these new converts have a "treasure" within them that we must contend for. Paul calls this a mystery "which has been hidden from ages and from generations, but now has been revealed to His saints. To them God willed to make known what are the riches of the glory of this mystery among the Gentiles; which is Christ in you, the hope of glory" (Colossians 1:26-27).

Jesus spoke these words, "You judge according to the flesh; I judge no one" (John 8:15), and Paul stated, "Therefore, from now on, we regard no one according to the flesh" (II Corinthians 5:16). We are being called upon to judge according to the Spirit and not according to the flesh. That doesn't mean we ignore, cover up or justify sin (including my own), but that we begin to lay hold of the truth that "greater is He that is in us than he that is in the world" (I John 4:4). If we really believe this, it will change the way we speak about ourselves and others (as well as our prayer lives). Let us be found following the lead of our

Master, "The words that I speak to you are spirit, and they are life". As believers we have a creative anointing upon our lives. When released, whether in word or deed, the anointing can literally change the atmosphere and spiritual climate thus making it easy for many to come to Christ and discover their purpose and destiny here on earth. It is time for the "treasures within" to be released upon the land.

5. *TRAINING:* Equipped for Church life vs. equipped for life

Let's consider the "last words" that Jesus uttered before He left this earth to return to His Father. This is better known to the Church as the "Great Commission", a mandate from the Lord Himself "to go forth and make disciples of all nations".

If there has been any one weak area in the Church, I believe it has been in the making of disciples (including my own fellowship). We have been quite proficient at making converts, but when it comes to making disciples, we have fallen short. Part of the reason for this is because of the cost in making disciples which requires an investment of time, resources, energy, etc. I believe another reason discipleship has been weak is that we have had no vision beyond the local church. Thus all of our "equipping" has been for church life, when in reality there are many in our midst who have been called to the "mountains of influence" that I referred to in the beginning of Chapter 7.

To be perfectly honest, we have only understood or accepted one part of the Master's plan, to make disciples. The part we have overlooked (or ignored) is the heart of the Father that all nations be discipled. He had the "nations" in mind when He redeemed His Church (Body) back to Him. There will be no reformation without the nations being discipled. Discipleship means being trained and equipped to be people of great influence in whatever mountain we are being called to serve on. That means equipping people for life (their purpose and destiny here on earth). What I am really talking about is five-fold disciples. Disciples who are:

Apostolic: know they have destiny for their lives and see the big picture.

Prophetic: fully aware they need to hear the voice of God and that they can.

Evangelistic: have a passion for the lost to get saved to fulfill their destiny.

Pastoral: know they have a call on their lives to serve, care and bless!

Teachers: know they can't survive without the "Word" (living Word)!

6. *RESPONSIBILITY*: Elders serving the pastor's vision vs. elders serving the vision

Once again, this subject becomes a little sensitive as we consider the role of the pastor. One of the weaknesses of having an unbiblical governmental structure is that the responsibility of setting the vision rests solely upon the pastor. In fact, he or she has been "hired" for such a responsibility. The problem that comes with this mindset is (1) the elders (or board) serve the pastor's vision and (2) it stifles the visions and dreams within the local body. Consequently, all resources and energy go towards supporting the pastors vision fulfilling only those called to the religion mountain. A Kingdom vision makes room for people to be expanded in their mountain of influence, a vision elders can easily serve and provide oversight to. This also places a demand upon the individual anointings giving great opportunity for Kingdom creativity to be released into the mountains of influence.

7. *GOVERANCE:* Staff (ministry) driven vs. being elder led

Paul writes these words to Titus (1:5), "For this reason I left you in Crete, that you should set in order the things that are lacking, and appoint elders in every city as I commanded you.." This was not just a "suggestion" to Titus, but a command! The apostle Paul understood something about church life that we have yet to grasp. I trust you have taken time to read and study chapter 5 which covers this area of governance. Wherever the pastor has been called to carry the responsibility of the vision, you will ultimately find the pastor and his/her staff driving the bus. We call this "ministry driven" where all events, functions, etc. are kept within the four walls of the church and very little emphasis is given to equipping and releasing people to the mountains of influence. So instead of the elders fulfilling the role and responsibility of leading, guiding, and protecting the flock, the responsibility falls upon the pastor and his or her staff.

8. *RELATIONSHIP:* What they can do vs. who they are

As you can see from the "church model" we have described above, the need for quality people to serve the pastor's vision is essential. Therefore, the question always becomes two-fold, "what are you able to do" and "how can that which you are able to do be used to serve my vision"? The answer to these two questions will determine the basis of the relationship. In a Kingdom model, the goal is to help the believer discover and value the "treasure within them" so they can be equipped and released into their mountain of influence, the vision God has deposited within them. The basis of relationship in the Kingdom model rests more on "who you are" rather than what you can do.

Let us be mindful that the treasure within enables each and every one of us to do things beyond that which we are capable of in the natural. It is the anointing within, which

God uses to do those things through us (earthen vessels) which only He can.

9. *CREATIVITY*: Being stifled vs. being released (taking ownership)

Let's take a moment and define creative as "having or showing an ability to make new things or think of new ideas".

Knowing that all of mankind is made in His image (the Creator Himself) means that every person has a "seed" of creativity within them. This powerful force (ability) that exists in the Church gives it the ability to tap into the creative power of God to bring forth new ideas, concepts, inventions, etc. It should be the heart and desire of the Church to see "creativity" unleashed upon the land and into the mountains of influence. Obviously, the "church model" does not serve creativity very well. However, the Kingdom model makes room for creativity to be released. Here are some of the characteristics of both models:

Church Model	Kingdom Model
1. Must serve pastor's vision……....limitless vision (7 mountains)	
2. Just room in local church………....unlimited room in the world	
3. Not everyone can fit (liability)……....many sizes/places (assets)	
4. Many casualties……………………....freedom to grow and go	
5. Freedom to go……………………………....freedom to return	

As we well know, in today's world of technology, creativity is being stirred in the hearts of people. As this "new wine" is being poured out, let us be found faithful in providing "new wine skins" for it to be poured into, lest it be wasted!

10. *EFFECTIVENESS:* Numbers vs. city transformation

As we well know, it is very natural in today's world to measure "success" by numbers. Unfortunately, the Church is not exempt from practicing the same principle. We must admit numbers are important, but as important as they are, they must not become the measuring stick for success. Once again, as we observe the two models (church vs. Kingdom), we discover one model seeks growth within while the other model seeks growth outside the church. That means the church model works at "making room" inside the four walls for growth while the Kingdom model acknowledges there is all kinds of room in the city (mountains) for growth. As you can see, the church model fosters "competition" (who is going to get the most numbers) while the Kingdom model fosters what we call "synergy". Please review chapter 6 where I address the "Synergy of the Ages" and its influence upon the world. Truly He is the measuring stick and His ways are much higher than ours!

11. *MISSION:* Bring them in vs. send them out

There is not much I can add to this one as we have covered it quite well in the previous ten points. However, it is quite clear by this time that the "mission" of the Church model is to bring them in (get them in the church). In reality, this is a lofty vision and one that pleases the Father. It is His will that none should perish but all get saved and connected to a local church. It is there they will be fed, nurtured, equipped, protected, find relationships, etc. However, without a Kingdom mindset in the church they will never understand or fulfill their purpose and destiny in this life. The Kingdom model church focuses on each person becoming whole, healed, and equipped so they can be "sent out" to be people of influence in the mountain they are called to. There is something organic about this that releases the creative potential in each person and the mission ultimately becomes city transformation.

12. *ACTIVITIES:* Dividing the generations vs. connecting the generations

As we have learned in previous chapters, God never intended for the generations to be disconnected. He is the Father of Abraham, Isaac, and Jacob. All throughout scripture we find one example after another of generations connecting to fulfill the purposes of God. That is still His heart. However, the church model is distinctively designed to "divide" the generations. Each generation has their "own table" they sit at tolerating one another and waiting for the opportune time to take charge. The enemy is very aware of this and does everything he can to keep the generations apart, knowing that if they begin to link arms and work together, nothing will be impossible for them. Bringing the generations together is much easier said than done. We each have our favorite style of ministry, music, preaching, governing, etc. The children sit at one table, teenagers at another table, the young adults have their own table, the middle age have their table, the semi-retired have their table and the retired (and older) have theirs. And might I add, all under the same roof. However, there is a growing awareness we will never be fruitful in discipling the nations without the synergy of generations being released upon the land. So instead of "passing the baton", let us "run together" to finish the course and finish it well. This will require humility and open hearts in each generation.

In 2009, there were two churches in the city of Minot, North Dakota, that decided to merge. They had much in common and shared similar values. As the leadership teams from both assemblies prayed and fasted concerning God's will for them, it became very apparent He wanted the two churches (Shiloh Christian Fellowship and Northland Harvest Church) to merge and become one. I can honestly say this has been a great "marriage" and most certainly the heart of the Father. However, one of the first things we had to address was the difference in worship styles, songs, etc. (which was more generational than individual churches). And as the senior leader, God spoke very clearly to me that I was to be intimately involved in this transition He was taking us through (even though I was not a worship leader or on the worship team). I must confess I like to sing and quite often get accused of singing too loudly (smile). Knowing I was being called to pastor this unique group of people (all musicians are unique) for a season until we were in unison (one voice), this was task I did not take lightly. After the second meeting we established a criterion (foundation) that we could build upon and one that has stood the test of time. In view of all the differences (worship style, songs, age, etc.), we came to a place that we could all agree on, and that was that "everyone involved had a pure heart". This willful decision made room for diversity and free expression, allowing the Holy Spirit to take these clay vessels and shape them into a unified worship team. The result was a release of sounds from heaven and a creativity that is heard not only in our city, state, and region, but also in the heavens. There is an incense of prayer and worship ascending to heaven (Revelation 5:8-9) that is releasing the "proceeding Word of the Lord" upon the land. This "word" is not returning void (Isaiah 55:11). This, my friend, is generational synergy and a fulfillment of Malachi 4:6. So instead of a "curse" upon the land, there is a "blessing"!

Chapter 9

UNDER RECONSTRUCTION

In the summer of 2011, the Souris River overflowed its banks as it moved through our city of Minot, North Dakota. It was considered a "100 year flood" and had a devastating effect upon our city and all the communities up and down the river. The Souris (also known as the Mouse River) flows into our state from Saskatchewan, Canada, dipping down into Minot and then back up into Canada (Manitoba).

Our church building (Northland Harvest) had the misfortune of being along the banks of the river and was inundated with six and one-half feet of water on the main floor that remained for almost three weeks. We were one amongst many in the city (including over 4000 homes) that were devastated, many never to be restored.

Many families have spent the last four years trying to recover so they could move back into their homes and businesses. After three weeks we were allowed to return to assess the damages which were way beyond anything you could think or imagine, including mud, silt, mold, and the stench of dead fish. We were faced with the choice to tear down or reconstruct our church building. We chose to reconstruct and after 15 months were able to move back in. Here are some lessons we learned as we walked through the "restoration process":

1. Restoration is not an event but a process.
2. It is not always easy to embrace the process (messy).
3. Time is a key factor whether it is "time spent" or "just waiting".
4. A sense of "community" is essential to finish the course (can't go alone).
5. Take time to celebrate the small things and the process.
6. The glory of the latter house is greater than the former.

We (the Church) are also under reconstruction and have been so since the Dark Ages (roughly 800 years). During Peter's second sermon (Acts 3:19-21), he confirms the fact that Christ's suffering was a fulfillment of prophecy and proceeds to call those present to "Repent, therefore and be converted, that your sins may be blotted out, so that times of refreshing may come from the presence of the Lord, that He may send Jesus Christ who was preached to you before, whom heaven must receive until the times of restoration of all things, which God has spoken by the mouth of all His holy prophets since the world began". We have the privilege of living in the restoration period, being reconstructed for His glory.

So let's do a short history lesson on the Church and what has taken place in the last 2000 years. It begins with a picture of the early Church being full of power and not confined to a building. Scriptures tell us that Paul and his company were accused of turning "the world upside down" (Acts 17:6). Now that's what I call being influential!

However, as we learn from Church history, within 100 years after the Church was born it began to lose its influence and started its downward spiral into that which is known as the Dark Ages (1200 AD).

1. 100 AD: no longer recognized apostolic grace
2. 130 AD: laying on of hands became a ritual
3. 140 AD: no longer recognized prophetic grace
4. 150 AD: the gifts of spirit were no longer relevant
5. 160 AD: plurality of elders ceased to exist
6. 180 AD: local church autonomy (identity) disappears
7. 200 AD: worship becomes a ritual and Body ministry ceases
8. 240 AD.: holiness is replaced by worldliness
9. 250 AD: water baptism ceases
10. 350 AD: salvation by faith disappears
11. 380 AD: Rome was made final authority in all church matters

After realizing what took place, it is not hard to understand why the Church entered into a thousand years of darkness. It wasn't until the reformer Martin Luther nailed his 95 Theses of Contention to the Wittenberg Church door that things began to change. It is also worthy to note that the last that was lost was the first to be restored.

1. 1517 AD: Justification by faith restored (Martin Luther)
2. 1524 AD: water baptism restored (Anabaptist movement)
3. 17th Century: emphasis on spiritual life restored
4. 1750 AD: holiness emphasis restored (John Wesley)
5. 19th Century healing restored
6. 1900 AD: baptism in the Holy Spirit restored

7. 1906 AD: spiritual gifts and ministries began to be restored
8. 1948 AD: laying on of hands and spontaneous praise restored

There is certainly more we could add to this list, but this gives you a little snapshot of the decline and restoration of the Church. As you can see, the Church morphed from a living organism into a dead institution. Once again, the restoration (or reconstruction) of the Church has been a lengthy process and deserves our attention as there are many things we can learn. I would like to take the last chapter and address the decline and fading influence of the five-fold ministry in the early Church and the profound effect it had in ushering in the Dark Ages. In so doing, we must keep in mind that the Church functioned as an "institution" for over 1000 years. That in and of itself has had a profound effect on the restoration process. The exciting part is that the Church is once again going through the restoration process and becoming a "living organism"!

Chapter 10

THE RESTORATION OF THE NEW TESTAMENT CHURCH

In the last chapter we did a brief history on the early Church and its decline into what is known as the Dark Ages. Even though the Church remained in the Dark Ages for over 1000 years, there remained a "remnant" that clung to the "truths" declared by the apostles of the early Church. Once again let's take a look at what happened with the five-fold ministry during the "falling away" and "restoration" of the Church.

Apostolic Grace

As we learned in the last chapter, apostolic grace ceased to exist towards the end of the first century (100 AD). The Church no longer honored the gift of the Apostle in its midst, resulting in a lack of vision beyond themselves. Scriptures (Proverbs 29:18) make it clear that people without a vision perish (cast off restraints); or as the Message Bible says "they stumble all over themselves".

Apostolic grace also carries a passion to see Christ's character formed in each believer. Those having this grace are fully aware that in order to see city transformation there has to be transformation in the Church to such degree that His character is being displayed wherever His people go. In the ceasing of the apostolic grace, lives are no longer being conformed to His image.

Where there is no desire to be conformed to His image you will also find no desire to search the scriptures to discover the hidden mysteries of Christ. The revelation of "Christ in you, the hope of glory" has nothing to attach itself to, thereby stunting the spiritual growth. The end result is the absence of apostolic grace to seek out and stir up the "treasures" within the earthen vessels. Because "spiritual fathers" are disappearing from the scene, God has no other recourse but to "strike the earth with a curse" (Malachi 4:6). Then we watch as the Church begins to tumble into the Dark Ages.

Prophetic Grace

As the apostolic grace begins to wane, so does the prophetic grace. By 140 AD there was no longer a "now word" of the Lord to be given or received. The end result of this was a "people without any vision" who ended up wandering in the wilderness without any restraints, just stumbling over themselves.

Teacher Grace

Next in line to disappear from the scene was the grace gifting of the "teacher". By this time we have a people who have no vision nor any desire to hear what God is saying. The condition of the Church was in such a state they were incapable of hearing the voice of the Lord. Without apostolic doctrine, the teachers end up having nothing to teach. Their desire for God's people to experience the "living word" is met with great resistance and unbelief. Remember, faith comes by hearing and hearing by the word of God (Romans 10:17). Now we have a people without any Biblical foundations who are celebrating their independence and freedom to do whatever they choose. The light continues to diminish becoming darker and darker.

Evangelistic Grace

By 300 AD, the Evangelists discover they have no Gospel to preach, nor any people who are willing to listen. There is no desire amongst the people to be saved, simply because they do not believe they are lost. In a short time the evangelistic grace dissipates from the scene and the season gets darker and darker. As society approaches the darkest hour, the doctrine of "salvation by faith only" disappears from the scene and man is left to himself.

Pastoral Grace

Because of "no truth", man was free to do whatever he wanted. The need for a pastoral gifting no longer existed. There was no one to shepherd as each person was wandering around doing his or her own thing. However, inherent within mankind is a desire to be led. "We want a king"! Because they had rejected King Jesus, another king (emperor) rose to the occasion. His name was Constantine!

Constantine became the emperor of Rome in 306 AD and ruled until 337 AD. This Roman Emperor had a soft spot in his heart for the Christians, probably because of his mother, Helena, as she was a professing Christian. During his reign, he issued the Edict of Milan (313 AD) legalizing Christian worship. He decreed Christianity as the dominant religion of the Roman Empire under "one condition"; that the Roman Government would serve as the final authority in all Church matters.

This paved the way for the Church of Rome and the first papacy making the Pope as the supreme head! So now, if you wanted to become a Christian you had to become a member of the Roman Empire qualifying you to become a member of the Roman Catholic Church. The Church remained in the Dark Ages for over a 1000 years. It wasn't until 1517 that the "restoration process" began and continues today.

The Restoration of the Church

In 1517, a man by the name of Martin Luther had dedicated himself to monastic life. His desire to please God through prayers, fastings, etc. only brought to him a keener awareness of his own sinfulness. It was during this time he set his heart to study the Scriptures. Luther discovered that words like "righteousness" and "penance" took on a new meaning. He also discovered the Church had wandered away from some key central truths which led him to put on paper his 95 Theses and nail to the church door at Wittenberg, accusing the Catholic church of heresy. This revelation of "the just shall live by faith" began the Protestant Reformation and was the first step in the restoration of the Church. "For by grace are you saved through faith, and that not of yourselves; it is the gift of God" (Ephesians 2:8).

Care Centered (Pastoral)

As restoration began to take place, the need for "pastoral grace" was once again ignited. People began to be aware of their need to be shepherded. Embracing Christ as the Way, the Truth, and the Life was met with great resistance due to the fact that the Church had been operating in a "works mentality" for over a 1000 years. The Church had become very independent and "change" was not welcomed. As the five-fold pastoral grace was being restored, the Church became more of a "Care Center" where people could be cared for, healed, and protected.

Lost Centered (Evangelistic)

As the wave of Protestant Reformation spread across the land, many people became aware of their lost condition. This made way for the "evangelistic grace" to once again come upon the scene. Becoming aware that there was only "one way" to heaven (which was through faith in the finished work of the cross), ignited the evangelistic spirit to once again preach the gospel of salvation. "Works" could no longer save you and never did. The only way to become a member of the Church was by accepting Jesus Christ as your Lord and Savior. As the pastor grace paved the way for "Care Centered churches", the evangelistic grace paved the way for "Lost Centered churches". Their passion to see sinners come to Christ created what is better known today as "evangelical churches". For several hundred years these two ingredients of caring and saving were the main focus for much of the church during its restoration process. Due to the spirit of independence, it seemed the previous movement always persecuted the next movement and they became "individual" movements in and of themselves. Without understanding and embracing the other five-fold ministries this will automatically happen. For example, the Care Centered churches will morph into "self-centered, in-grown" expressions without the other ministries. The Lost Centered churches will turn into predominantly evangelistic centers that will be weak in the word and all resources will go towards evangelism.

Word Centered (Teachers)

As the evangelistic grace was reintroduced to the Church, there became a great need for the Word to be taught. This paved the way for the "teacher grace". In the early 1970's, a number of "Word Centered churches" began to arise. But once again, there never seemed to be a reaching out or embracing of the different movements. This led to churches which were strong in doctrine, overriding relationships and moving into legalism. Much of the time when "present day truth" was presented, it fell on deaf ears and was rejected because it came out of the Word movement.

Revelation Centered (Prophetic)

As "truths" are being restored to the Church, we also see the revelation and need for five-fold ministry to be restored. The problem we face is that in the restoration process all five-fold ministries remain independent of one another. With the restoration of the teacher grace came the restoration of the "prophetic grace". In the 1980's and 90's we began to hear more about this particular grace and its ability to disturb the "comfort zone" of many. As you recall, the prophetic grace has a great passion for the Church to hear and receive the "now word" of the Lord. The question becomes "what is the Lord speaking to the Church in this hour"?

This grace gifting helps the Church discover the direction it needs to be moving in. Now that the teacher grace is back in the saddle, the "now word" can be expounded upon. But once again, many Revelation (prophetic) Centered churches chose the road of independence and fell into serious error. Without the balance of the other five-fold gifts, prophetic people lean towards everything being "black & white" and the main message becomes "repent". Obviously, prophecy plays a very important role in what God is doing today. Once again, without the balance of the other ministries, it is very easy to find yourself living (or dying) on the prophetic word. They (like the rest of the five-fold gifts) are not meant to function alone and are in great need of the apostolic grace.

Vision Centered (Apostolic)

In the early 1980's I was introduced to partial understanding and revelation of the apostolic grace. It was a new concept and in some circles classified as a cult. Yet I knew it was a Biblical term as well as a gift that was essential for the Church to fulfill its destiny here on earth. Those with this grace upon them were "visionary" people and had an ability to see the big picture. They seemed to never lack vision which quite often became their downfall. Often times the "independent" spirit prevailed. In their far-sightedness and unwillingness to submit to the other grace giftings, they found themselves promoting their own vision instead of His. In order to protect their vision, it could only be done "their way". If you were not willing to do it their way, then you must get out of the way. There seemed to be no thought or concern for those who might get trampled on along the way. Once again, it seemed as though the spirit of independence had prevailed. Is there any hope for the restoration of the Church? With great confidence, I can emphatically say "YES"!

Earlier in chapter nine, I made reference to Peter's second sermon in Acts 3:19-21, where he addresses "times of refreshing coming from the presence of the Lord" and the fact that "heaven must receive Christ until the times of restoration of all things". This means that Christ will not be returning to earth until the restoration of all things! As we have learned, those things that were lost as the Church passed through the Dark Ages have been restored back to the Church. The problem, (and not a small one at that), the Church has faced during the restoration process is the "spirit of independence" which is currently breaking down. There is an understanding coming to the Church and its leaders that we cannot fulfill our Kingdom destiny here on earth without the wider Body of Christ. The Church will never come into the "unity of the faith and the knowledge of the Son of God, to a perfect (mature) man, to the measure and stature of the fullness of Christ" until the five-fold grace giftings begin working together and not independently of one another (Ephesians 4:11-16).

I believe I am seeing this happen (at least in part) in my life and have great confidence the Church is entering its finest hour. As we respond to Him and His desires, we are going to experience in a much greater measure, "times of refreshing from the presence of the Lord". He is building His house and the gates of hell will not prevail for it has been designed by Him and is being built by Him "TO LAST" forever, and ever, and ever.

Jesus is coming back for a Church (people) who have apostolic vision. This people will avail themselves to hearing and obeying the now word from heaven in preparation for the greatest harvest of all times. Because of their desire to know the Word (written and living), the love of God will so abound in their hearts, they will become living epistles shedding abroad the love of God upon a sick and dying world. THE BRIDE IS MAKING HERSELF READY! (Revelation 19:7) It is time for the marriage supper of the Lamb!

A LAST WORD.....

In closing I am reminded of Paul's admonition to the church in Corinth (I Corinthians 1:10,11).."According to the grace of God which was given to me, as a wise master builder I have laid the foundation, and another builds upon it. But let each one take heed how he builds on it. For no other foundation can anyone lay than that which is laid, which is Jesus Christ".

The next four verses make it very clear that "each one's work" is going to be tested by fire. Unless we come into alignment with not only His will...but His way, there will be the suffering of great loss. Our response in this hour to the Chief Corner Stone (Jesus Christ) is critical to the fulfillment of the Great Commission (Matthew 28:18-20).

"Holy Spirit, grant us understanding of the times we are living in that we might know what to do and how to build (I Chronicles 12:32) that You Father, would be glorified and that the renown of Your name would be known and displayed throughout the earth". AMEN!

Contact information: howthenshallwebuild@gmail.com

32355590R00057

Made in the USA
San Bernardino, CA
03 April 2016